"It's not too early to be thinking about the year 2050—especially how to help today's generation of children become resilient disciples of Jesus, ready to lead the church while engaging and influencing the culture. This could be the most strategic conversation for the church today."

John C. Maxwell
New York Times Best-Selling Author, Leadership Expert, Speaker

---

"Valerie Bell invites us all into a conversation about what faith looks like when today's kids are tomorrow's adults. So much has changed in the past 30 years, but wait until you see the next 30. In the midst of that ever-changing environment, Valerie points out this one reality that remains: having a consistent, caring leader in the life of a child is still the greatest determiner of that child's spiritual future. Don't miss her insights into what will make the difference for every kid and every family."

Reggie Joiner
Founder and CEO, Orange

"*RESILIENT* is a sobering wake-up call for the church, but even more than that, it provides God-inspired hope and a pathway for all Jesus followers to lead today's emerging generation into resilient intimacy with Jesus, one life at a time. If the church answers the call, no doubt it will prevail more in the next generation than ever before."

Santiago "Jimmy" Mellado
President and CEO, Compassion International

"The next 30 years will be the largest gospel opportunity in the history of America, and *RESILIENT* is important because it encourages every parent, pastor and adult to be fearless as we rethink how we love and disciple the future of the church."

Joshua Crossman
CEO Pinetops Foundation; Author of *The Great Opportunity: The American Church in 2050*

"When an immensely gifted author writes about a critically important subject, the result is a singularly significant book. In this case Valerie Bell is that author and this is that book. Valerie and team's urgent love for children and timely concern for The Church makes every page of RESILIENT interesting and indispensable. This is a must read for anyone who cares about our children and who is willing to be moved to create a preferred future for them and our world."

Terry A. Smith, Lead Pastor
The Life Christian Church in West Orange, NJ and Author of *The Hospitable Leader*

Printed in the United States of America

First Printing, 2020

ISBN 9781946680648

Walsworth Publishing Company
803 S Missouri Ave
Marceline, MO 64658

RESILIENT

CHILD DISCIPLESHIP AND
THE FEARLESS FUTURE OF THE CHURCH

VALERIE BELL

CHRIS MARCHAND | MATT MARKINS | MIKE HANDLER

TABLE OF CONTENTS

DEAR CHILD,

You are little for such a short time. But, when you grow up and think back on your childhood, we hope some of your earliest memories are about us, the church. Before you could walk or talk, you probably remember someone at church—even if you don't remember who, exactly—rocking you and singing sweet songs into your fears until your tears were dried. Sitting in a circle with other kids, someone is singing *Jesus Loves Me* to you. It is probably one of the first songs you will learn to sing.

Today you lisp your way through John 3:16, *For God so loved the world that he gave his only begotten son, that whosoever believeth in him should not perish, but have eternal life* (KJV). But this verse (along with many others) is being committed to your memory where it will dwell for years, informing your entire lifetime. You will remember laughter that filled that special kid-friendly place at church and how it became your happy place with other kids every week.

Today we celebrate your childhood among us! In rooms painted with childrens' delight in mind and furnished with tables and chairs that are just-your-size, you hear the Good News of the gospel and come to Jesus with childlike faith and trust. Your belief is nurtured by a community that protects your earliest understanding of God's love and demonstrates it to you.

We are the church and you, child, are precious to us.

We are your Sunday school teachers ... the ones with the funny puppets and great smiles. We are the people who run your KidMin programs, whose faith is so strong and so accessible that you easily embrace God's love because you can see it in us. We hope you remember us, the adults who show up every week to make sure the church is there for you.

All is fine for now, but there is a rub: you are growing up and today is not the final chapter. Soon you will be an adult, living in a world that is yet unknown to any of us, but a world whose challenges to faith are even now rising on the horizon. As an adult, will your child-like faith hold strong against the secular world's embrace of political correctness, relativism that challenges absolute truth and sexual and gender choices without boundaries?

Your future looks challenging. Warm-fuzzy memories may not be enough to strengthen you then. Will we regret that we filled the small amount of time we had with you with delightful things, spiritual entertainment, but things so inconsequential they didn't travel into your adult life except as lovely memories?

Have we loved and entertained you, or have we also created disciples? With your adult future in mind, are we intentionally raising you to become Christ following men and women with both spine and heart—spine to stand firm for your Christian beliefs in an increasingly hostile secular world and heart to embrace that same intolerant-of-faith world, with a love that can't be ignored.

Will you grow up and be grateful that we, the church, gave you everything you needed to both lead the church and influence the culture? Will you be prepared because the church today anticipated the challenges you would face as Christian adults in 2050? Will you experience our love then, or will our brand of kid-friendly-for-today love fail you as adults?

The pages that follow are a love letter to your grown-up selves and the church's future. It is a strategy and blueprint for influencing a world we see coming your way. If you read it in the years to come, know that you were not only loved as children, but loved by the church who prepared you for your challenging adult years and tried to give you everything you needed to stand proud and unafraid.

May you know we never stopped loving you. And may that love root you firmly and prepare you for the decades to come when you are the church.

The future of the church rests with you.

I WANT YOU TO LOVE JESUS FOR THE REST OF YOUR LIFE

CHAPTER 1

A young teenage boy dressed for a typical day of school: gym shoes, T-shirt, shorts and stands center in the frame. No news here. But look closer. His head is bowed. He is praying. And most noticeably, he is praying alone. On a day called *See You at the Pole*™ when Christian kids across the world gather together at their school's flagpoles to publicly pray, Hayden stands at his school's flagpole utterly alone. That's how he captured our hearts.

At first, Hayden said he thought the other kids were simply late. So he bowed his head and waited for his friends to join him. But as the minutes slowly passed, no one came. He was solo. And publicly so. Exposed. Abandoned. Maybe a little embarrassed. At these crucial points in life, when Plan A folds, I'm guessing most people would walk away. Then later many of us would probably have a few choice words for our "friends" who didn't show up. Typically, these things end badly.

But Hayden did not fold. He did not leave. When Plan A went bust, he had the grit to move to Plan B.

His mother, Stacy Philpot, shared Hayden's thoughts on her blog:

> Hayden told me that as he stood alone and prayed the cry of his heart had been, "God as people drive by let them wonder, let their hearts be pricked." Eventually, when he realized that no one else was coming, the cry of his heart changed. He asked that God would do something with his standing alone.

IF A PICTURE IS WORTH A THOUSAND WORDS, THEN THIS PICTURE IS WORTH MILLIONS.

Most of us have prayed something like, "God, do something with Plan B. Do something with this publicly embarrassing situation. Do something with my aloneness. Please, do something with this mess. Show Yourself mighty."

When God's eyes searched the earth that day looking for those whose hearts were right towards Him, it seems that He must have seen Hayden. Because ...BOOM! Hayden's picture went viral and it's easy to think that God smiled along with the rest of us. In a Christian world concerned about the spiritual tenacity of Hayden's generation, his picture resonated with hope that there is a ***resilient remnant***—kids who will hold on to their faith no matter what. Hayden's response to all of this? "It's crazy because it's as if God answered in this big way!"

His mother's wonder is clear:

> *The little boy I'd rocked to sleep in blue airplane pajamas when he was sick. The toddler who loved Elmo and couldn't go to sleep without holding his Veggie Tales characters in his hands had captured the attention of our community by standing alone, by doing everything we'd ever taught him, everything we'd ever hoped he would do. I was completely undone.*

Hayden is resilient.

So that's what this book examines: spiritual resilience—how it is nurtured and developed in children or a generation of kids. We are especially looking at resilience with a long view, through the lens of 2050 when today's children will be adults.

Like Hayden's mom, will we be exclaiming with wonder over our children then, "You are doing everything we've ever taught you? Everything we'd ever hoped you would do?" Or will we mourn over empty churches and regret that we could have done more?

We ask questions today in hopes of fanning the flames of the fearless future of faith through the discipleship of today's kids. We strongly believe that child discipleship is the most crucial conversation impacting the future of faith: we must pursue the discipleship of today's kids with resilience as a goal.

Many contributors have helped form the thoughts in this book. We share a common desire—to come alongside parents, pastors and KidMin leaders to help raise generations of children who identify with Christ publicly and without apology—kids who as adults will be resilient disciples despite the obstacles and disapproval of our culture.

THIS BOOK ASKS MANY QUESTIONS:

Are our kids becoming Christian disciples, or is the culture engulfing them?

Are we preparing kids to function as Christ followers in this culture, or is our guidance better fit for a previous past culture?

Are we effectively engaging this culture or being silenced by it?

Are we protecting our kids rather than preparing them to engage a post-Christian culture?

At Awana, we are asking ourselves these questions. And more. As a result, we are refocusing a robust 70-year-old ministry to kids in order to address the long-view questions around resilience. [1]

Are we preparing today's kids to lead the church and influence the culture in 2050?

Are we simply raising up Bible memory champions assuming they are disciples?

Have kids taken a second place to curriculum or programming?

Are we about achievement or resilience? Or can we emphasize both?

At Awana we have committed to owning our need to refocus a 70 plus year-old-ministry. Please understand, our bottom line is not simply to promote the Awana brand. Obviously, we care about this ministry immensely. But even more than that, our passion is to ignite a movement of God that starts in the children's wing of the church and spreads to the pews and out into the streets—a spiritual awakening all across North America and beyond!

Our "front row" experience as practitioners and the conclusions we have made has been further validated by research data. But the best research in the world goes nowhere unless it is picked up by practitioners. The ball is in our court and we are ready to pick it up. Two timely research perspectives stand out. In *Faith for Exiles: Five Ways for a New Generation to Follow Jesus in a Digital Age*, the Barna Group provides data that informs our experience as practitioners—whether we are church leaders, KidMin directors and volunteers or parents. [2]

We also have benefited from the work of Ed Stetzer who serves as the executive director of the Billy Graham Center at Wheaton College. His cultural navigation in the book *Christians in the Age of Outrage: How to Bring Our Best When the World is at Its Worst* has been an enormous help. [3]

What are these voices telling us? The data and analysis from both of these sources points to a shrinking population of young Christians. Barna describes these young disciples as "Jesus followers who are resiliently faithful in the face of cultural coercion and who live a vibrant life in the Spirit." [4] Pointing to the last decade's sobering dropout rate of 59 to 64 percent of church kids they state, "If our young people are going to thrive in digital Babylon, they have to move beyond familiarity with Jesus to a place of intimacy." [5]

In addition to the alarming drop out rate, the Barna Group asks how many Christian young people meet the resilient discipleship criteria? Their research indicates there is a counter cultural 10 percent of young Christians whose faith is vibrant and robust. . .this number represents just under four million 18 to 20-year-olds in the U.S. who follow Jesus and are resiliently faithful." [6] David Kinnaman and Mark Matlock of the Barna Group call this 10 percent of church kids Resilient Disciples.

And while four million resilient disciples represent an impressively resilient spiritual group, it is a remnant. A piece of the potential. A small fraction. A minority of the kids the church touches. Or bringing that figure home: A few of our grandkids, but not most. Some of our children but more who are not in that category than are. What child of "yours" would you not be heart broken to lose? The small size of this group who buy in spiritually should definitely concern all of us.

But retention is not the only challenge to the future of faith. In the United States we are experiencing a cultural shift away from Christianity like we have never seen before. This is huge. The group who checks the "None" box on religious preferences is growing and becoming more influential. Ed Stetzer helps us understand this cultural shift away from "Convictional Christianity." "We can try to reclaim a cultural norm (Mainstream Judeo-Christian consensus) that is dying if not already dead. Or we can grasp the central truth of the moment in which we live, understanding the challenges and opportunities Christians face in this new culture.

"We have to consider both the moment we are in and the mission we are on." [7]

Stetzer's chart, on the following page, captures "the moment we are in and the moment we will be in"—a progressive shift away from Christian values in our U.S. culture and the ensuing cultural divide. It shows the direction of cultural influence in our country. In the future, there will be Convictional Christians.

IF OUR YOUNG PEOPLE ARE GOING TO THRIVE IN DIGITAL BABYLON, THEY HAVE TO MOVE BEYOND FAMILIARITY WITH JESUS TO A PLACE OF INTIMACY

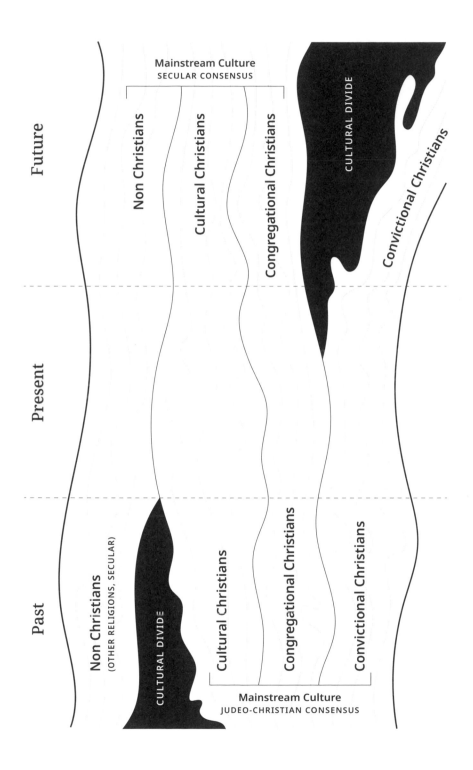

Future

Mainstream Culture
SECULAR CONSENSUS

Non Christians

Cultural Christians

Congregational Christians

CULTURAL DIVIDE

Convictional Christians

Present

Past

Non Christians
(OTHER RELIGIONS, SECULAR)

CULTURAL DIVIDE

Cultural Christians

Congregational Christians

Convictional Christians

Mainstream Culture
JUDEO-CHRISTIAN CONSENSUS

 Christians in the Age of Outrage: How to Bring our Best When the World is at its Worst, Ed Stetzer, used by permission

Resilient Disciples. Convictional Christians. Each name represents a group that is what we are calling the Resilient Remnant.

At Awana, we have been leaders in the spiritual training of kids and youth for over 70 years. Our front row seat to church health and trends led us to the same conclusions as Barna and Stetzer. Our exit polls with churches leaving Awana are almost universal in reporting that the church's number one problem in the discipleship of their children is the lack of volunteers. In some cases, the church has grown apathetic to its own future. We have also watched and experienced the downside of the church going "Sunday only" and dropping KidMin programming to an hour or so a week, a solution for the "immediate" that, in our opinion, is short-ranged and will be hard pressed to create the kind of discipleship needed for 2050.

But we are also far from quitting. Far from it. For the sake of the 2050 church, the future of faith and the influence of this country, we are focusing on nurturing and expanding the Resilient Remnant, Convictional Christians or what Barna calls Resilient Disciples.

So what is spiritual resilience?

```
Spiritual Resilience

A quality that describes the spiritual elasticity of a
child or adult. The resistant strength to bend and flex,
but not break against the weight of culture.
```

Resilience is the muscle discipleship builds.

We want to be clear: We are not promoting a particular brand called Awana as the solution. We are actually in the process of examining our own ministry and making critical shifts in our approach with 2050 in mind. We are retooling in order to nurture kids' faith by doing everything possible today to prepare them to meet the challenges of not only today, but also of tomorrow.

66

**WE STRONGLY BELIEVE
THAT CHILD DISCIPLESHIP
IS THE MOST CRUCIAL
CONVERSATION IMPACTING
THE FUTURE OF FAITH ..."**

Our intention is to further a conversation about discipleship and the future of faith. We realize this conversation needs many perspectives. Our goal is to invite everyone into this crucial discussion. Welcome Lifeway! Welcome Orange! Welcome denominations! Welcome academia and researchers! Come talk! Come pray! Come strategize! Come together and make a strong stand for discipleship in the rising tide of cultural secularization.

RESILIENCE IS THE MUSCLE DISCIPLESHIP BUILDS

I, like many of you, am a child of the church. We can look back at our childhoods as a study in discipleship. Why did we stay? What was it that helped us identify with Jesus and His church as we grew up?

Years ago my niece hand-delivered a business card to me from someone she had met. The sender was Dr. Dr. John A. Martin, President of Roberts Wesleyan College. No that's not a typo. He has two doctorates. We were childhood friends, but college, marriage, family and careers had sent us in separate directions. Now, hearing from him after decades, I was reminded that our friendship was of a competitive nature. Who did better on the California Achievement tests? (National tests given to schoolchildren in the 50's...He did!) Who had the best report cards? (That would also be him!) Who ran the fastest? (Well, I beat him once in fourth grade!) Had I known he was going to be Dr. Dr. when he grew up, I would have chosen a more easily defeated sparring friend. So in the spirit of our competitive friendship as kids, I emailed him back.

"What's this Dr. Dr. business? Didn't I used to be smarter than you?"

But we shared more than a competitive relationship with each other. We shared the experience of being different. John's father was the dean of faculty at Moody Bible Institute and my father was the chairman of Moody's music department. John's father was my father's boss. Moody used to have a pledge for faculty that their families were expected to embrace as well. No movies. No alcohol. No dancing. No smoking. All were considered worldly and potentially sinful by our parents' generation of evangelicals. Every year when John and I were in elementary school our mothers would write similar notes:

To Whom it May Concern,

Please excuse my son John, (or my daughter Valerie) from the dancing in gym class this year. It is against our religious practices.

Thank you,

Mrs. Martin or Mrs. Burton

Our teachers would then place two small metal folding chairs on the sidelines and from there we would watch our friends and classmates square dance with each other. Although I had become a Christian as a preschooler, I began my discipleship in dance class! Being sidelined had much more to do with my father keeping his job than my religious convictions. Left to myself, I would have danced. No doubt about it. It was a discipline I often resented.

But I had begun to identify with my parents' beliefs beyond their non-dancing policy. I belonged to something more meaningful than square dancing. Even though it meant sitting it out and being sidelined, it also meant I belonged to Jesus and to His people. Clearly the definitions of spirituality that belonged to my parents' generation as worldly avoidances were not the motivators behind my budding spirituality. They simply put me in a different category of young people. As I grew up, I was never asked to a school dance or parties where there might be dancing. I was socially sidelined by my embrace of my parents' spiritual disciplines and definitions of worldliness. But I found belonging in other places. I found great joy in growing spiritually with other kids my age. At school, when they teased me sometimes and called me a Holy Roller or a Bible Banger, my identity in Christ was already firmly in place. Their words did not wound me.

My senior yearbook tells the story of my high school discipleship journey. In an irony of ironies (and boy, did they have their nerves after everything they put me through), my class voted me the "Ideal Girl." What? Does that seem odd to anybody besides me? And what I remember of Dr. Dr. was that he was the most respected boy in our class. We were favored even though we were different. We were becoming disciples.

I doubt we would have chosen that path of identity without our parents' strong guidance, but in time, we each chose to be disciples of Jesus and that has made all the difference.

What do I know personally about resilience? Resilience is learned. It is not automatic. It comes through discipline and identities built in Christ. The disciplines that form resilience are hard. It means we will not be "them." We will be "other." We will stand alone at flagpoles. We will sometimes "sit it out." We will be misunderstood and interpreted at the lowest levels. But we will have another kind of belonging that strengthens our spiritual spine and softens our hearts towards a lost world. We will know and love Jesus.

After serving on the Awana Board of Directors for four years, in 2016, I was pulled up from the board to become the CEO of Awana. At that moment I remembered those metal chairs on the sidelines where Dr. Dr. and I sat and my heart embraced the millions of children who we are calling around this world to the hard path of Christian discipleship. I knew I would be a part of calling them to be different, to be other, to experience so many variations on those little metal chairs. We are teaching them to be blameless and innocent, children of God without blemish in the midst of a crooked and twisted generation, among whom you shine as lights in the world. (Philippians 2:15, ESV). And more. Jesus calls them to give up their lives. To follow Him completely. To be his disciples totally.

I also remembered that on my pathway to developing my own identity when my sixth grade teacher asked me what I wanted to be when I grew up. I told him I wanted to be a lawyer for children. He smiled and told me there wasn't such a thing.

He was only partially right. There was Awana, the perfect place for a woman whose heart beat early and throughout her life for children. Awana is where some of the most dedicated, passionate advocates for children and the gospel I have ever met have given their lives. When I became Awana's CEO, I felt like I was like coming home. Here is where I belong...with other highly-dedicated child disciple makers and advocates for kids.

I am thrilled to have Chris Marchand, Matt Markins and Mike Handler contributing to this project as well. Chris is the Vice President, Partner Solutions. He is responsible for overseeing all of our curriculum development at Awana. Matt is Awana's President and Chief Strategy Officer. We call Mike Handler the extension of all of our right brains. Otherwise he's known as Awana's Chief Communications Officer. But above everything, they all have a passion for generations of kids to truly know God, and for the church and faith to thrive into 2050. I am honored to share this project with them.

I can't end this chapter without sharing a conversation I had with one of my grandsons. Rhys was six at the time. He had been a "failure to thrive" newborn. After the NICU doctors had exhausted their medical interventions and his digestive system was still as if it was asleep, they decided there was little more they could do. Rhys was put in a dark room to slow his body processes in hopes of prolonging his life. Our family was brokenhearted, but we asked for 24/7 access to Rhys. We prayed over that little body. We rocked and sang songs to him as if we could will him to keep living. When they sent him home, it was not to live, but to die surrounded by family.

We were on our own.

But he didn't die! He lived and thrived I might add. He still seems like a miracle to us. Through the years, we have noticed an unusual spiritual sensitivity with him. I've always wondered if that might be from all the prayers that were prayed over every cell of his baby body in his first weeks.

But back to the conversation we had. He asked me, "Lovie (my grandma name) have you ever heard God talk to you?"

That got my attention!

"Rhys do you mean have I heard him out loud? No, I never have. Have you?" I admit I was thinking, *Brace yourself, Lovie!*

This is what he said:

"Last night after everyone was asleep, I was still awake. I couldn't sleep. I felt a hand on my shoulder. I couldn't see anything, but I suddenly felt really, really happy."

Now I was intrigued.

"Then God talked to me," Rhys smiled.

"What did God say to you?"

He said, "I want you to love Jesus for the rest of your life."

In 2050 Rhys will be 39. Whether or not Rhys heard from God that night, I can't say for sure, but I can say these words reflect God's heart for this whole generation of children. There is a familiar biblical pattern here: Eli heard God's voice through young Samuel. A grandmother recognizes God's truth through her young grandson.

Could God be speaking to me through my young grandson? Perhaps. However, I do believe He wants me to tell this generation of church kids what He told Rhys:

"I want you to love Jesus for the rest of your lives."

ESSENTIAL QUESTIONS:

Are we winning or losing our kids?

Is the culture engulfing them?

What about the ones who stop showing up or fade away in their adult years? Do we let them slip away without an attempt to reintroduce them to Christ?

Are we preparing kids to function as Christ followers in **this** *culture, or is our guidance better fit to a previous better-known-to-us culture?*

Are we effectively engaging this culture or being silenced by it?

And is our silence impacting our kids' choices?

Are we protecting our kids **from** *rather than preparing them* **to** *engage a post-Christian culture?*

2050 AND THE FEARLESS FUTURE OF FAITH

CHAPTER 2

It's Monday night and I am walking my grandsons through the church parking lot.

Rowan (8), Rhys (6), Merrick (3), and I hold hands as we weave through the car labyrinth until we reach the safety of the sidewalk. They stay close to me, without being obviously clingy (they are, after all, boys!), but ask in whispers, "Lovie, are you going to stay with us for the rest of the night?"

Every week my answer is the same, "Of course, I will."

But this night is different. Rowan's little boy hand pulls away from me. Suddenly, he's running ahead with his two younger brothers sprinting in his wake.

Ah! My heart jumps. I can read this body language. Their feet pound out a pattern on the pavement I recognize. It's anticipation. It's joy. It's rushing to receive. In just a few weeks, they've learned what waits for them inside the church doors: something wonderful!

The greeters know them by name and welcome them with smiles.

"Hi, buddy! Glad you came Rhys."

"Good to see you Rowan. Whadcha do ... grow a couple of inches this week?"

"Hi, Merrick! Cool shoes you got there, man!"

THEIR FEET POUND OUT A PATTERN ON THE PAVEMENT I RECOGNIZE. IT'S ANTICIPATION. IT'S JOY. IT'S RUSHING TO RECEIVE.

It is warm and fun. There is food of course, because it is church after all! But there are precious intangibles as well; the walls ring with adult reassurances that life is sweet and God is love and peanut butter prayers and lisped Bible memory verses echo back in childish voices.

My grandkids belong to this tribe of children. Here is safety, wisdom and life direction. And more: here is a unique presence of loving, caring adults. Every week these kids make friends. Every week they fall in love with Jesus and His Word just a little bit more. I can see a precious work of God being formed more beautifully in their hearts. One grandson listens to the Bible every night as he falls to sleep. Another says he wants to marry a woman who is a "Jesus follower." And then there is the one who, when I told him I wanted him to grow up to be a spiritual giant, answered, "Yes. I'm going to be God." He's three. He thinks that's the best spiritual giant he can emulate. Yikes! At least, we still have time to work on that theology. But, right or wrong, they are forming, and we have plenty to discuss!

This life blessing of belonging that is rooted in a spiritual community is what I want for them. Desperately! One day they will look to me for reassurance (You're going to stay with us for the rest of our lives, aren't you Lovie?) and I won't be able to respond, "Of course, I will." When they let go of my hand for the last time, I hope they will joyfully face their tomorrows with confidence, knowing that everything they need in life has been given to them already and anything beyond is theirs for the asking. I hope they will hear the echo of my voice.

"Run with power, Rowan! Tap into your spiritual wisdom! Be resilient!"

"Go for it with joy, Rhys! The joy of the Lord is your strength."

"Take it by storm and don't be afraid, Merrick! God is your helper. Be fearless and run right into the center of the storm."

Remember my loves. Remember.

Hopefully, they will still have a wonderful church. Inside the walls of that ancient gathering they will be known by name and smiled on. There they will find their familiar tribe, their known God and His ever-more-applicable Word. And when they face uncertainty, loss or pain—which they certainly will—they will know to run to the church where they will be reminded that life is sweet, that God is love, and that this is where they belong.

Consider this: the present is more than the present. It is the foundation for the future. In 2050 these dearly loved grandchildren, along with your children and grandchildren, will be adults. This tribe of size 4s and 6s currently in Sunday schools and KidMin programs today will be the future leaders of the church, the salt in an increasingly secular culture, the people called to love and shine in a world that is becoming more openly hostile towards their beliefs, their place in the world and their God. The year 2050, by anyone's guess, is going to be tough on believers and the church.

If the future of faith is a kid singing *Jesus Loves Me* today, will that child be determinedly resilient and fearlessly ready to face his or her adult world? Will she be faithful?

Will today's church children be strong enough in their adult years to lead the church and influence the culture in which they must live in 2050?

Or will they be driven underground and muted?

Can discipleship be customized for their futures and the distinctive times in which they will be living?

Will we have given them the unique discipleship foundation they need to be leaders of that future mid-century church and will that foundation help them fearlessly engage the culture and influence it?

Today's church kids are growing up in both a secular and church culture that are unlike the cultures in which most adults grew up. More importantly the culture kids are experiencing is unlike the ones that are to come. I fear our assumptions of "sameness"—our cluelessness in the midst of huge cultural shifts—may lead us to be unresponsive to the needs these shifts present in building strong and relevant spiritual foundations for the years ahead.

WE ARE LIVING IN TIMES OF UNPRECEDENTED CHANGE.

The Barna Group makes this point as well:

> "In some ways, the church is not preparing young disciples for the world as it is. Cultural discernment is about teaching them not just what to think but also how to live. We must prepare them for the world as it truly is, not as we wish it to be." [1]

I fear we may realize too late that we gave them things that didn't really matter, things that didn't travel into their adult lives as anything more than spiritual entertainment and moralistic stories, things lacking real spiritual power and proactive purpose.

We are living in times of unprecedented change. The entire world is shifting and tilting towards an unknown future. And when it comes to our children, it is as if we are launching a generation of kids to land in 2050 on an unknown and faraway planet. How can we possibly prepare them to survive and thrive in that foreign 2050 place? This we sense: the adults of the future church will need to be disciples as few modern generations before them have had to be. They will need fearless resilience.

None of us knows the future with certainty, but we can look at some growing trends and see how these seismic shifts are impacting today's kids and foreshadowing their futures.

SCREEN DISCIPLESHIP

This first seismic shift: technology has brought a heightened velocity of secular culture. It points to several troubling emerging issues: a decline in well-being, a rise of addictive behavior among adults and adolescents and an engulfment in secular values.

Technology has brought us many advances and changed nearly every area of our lives, from how we learn, to how we travel, and how we relate to each other. It has saved us time and increased our productivity. But it has come at a cost that we are just now beginning to understand. As children use mobile technology, scientific research is beginning to tell us these screens are changing the brain functioning in ways we haven't seen before. After years of screen use, this huge social experiment as it were, the brain science data is now mature and substantive enough to report on the effects of kid's early exposure to the screen. Kids' screen usage puts the brain on pause developmentally. [2]

It's as if a media tsunami has engulfed our lives. The most current screen-usage trends can be seen to the right. [3]

Should we be concerned about this? A first-of-its-kind study by the Cincinnati Children Research Group reports, "It's clear that children who have too much screen time can have deficits in other areas, like language, imagination and emotions. The years from

Are we okay with this?

Average daily screen usage:

50 minutes
0-8 years old

6 hours
8-12 years old

9 hours
teenagers

THE WORLD OF SIN THAT WAS ONCE "OUT THERE"... HAS RETURNED WITH A VENGEANCE INTO THE PALM OF OUR KIDS HANDS.

three to five represent a formative stage of development. Too much screen time is a setup for atrophy, or underdevelopment of these higher-order brain networks. The brain just doesn't have to do any work. It will be harder for kids with underdeveloped networks to learn. It's like the lights are on, but nobody is home." [4]

Not only is technology compromising our brain formation and occupying large portions of our time, it is suspected of being the primary driver behind the deterioration of our mental health, especially our kids' mental health. Teens whose lives are dominated by mobile technology ... playing video games, texting and using social media are experiencing a significant and alarming plunge in emotional well-being compared to their less media-engaged peers. [5]

In a study charting well-being among American adolescents (measured by self-esteem, life satisfaction, and happiness), psychologists discovered a significant decline after 2012. In exploring the underlying causes, researchers observed that increased use of smartphones by teenagers is likely a contributor to the trend. They found that teenagers who spent more time engaged in screen activities (i.e., social media, the Internet, texting, and gambling) registered lower levels of psychological well-being. On the other hand, teenagers who limited smartphone use and regularly engaged in off screen activities such as in-person social interactions, sports or exercise, homework, and church activities had higher psychological well-being. [6]

The world of sin that was once "out there," that world that followers of Christ once practiced separation from—movies, smoking, drinking, drugs, etc.—has returned with a vengeance into the palm of our kid's hands.

Pornography, graphic musical lyrics, X-rated violent movies, extreme materialism, explicit sexting and a worldview that is opposite of and opposed to all things Christian. The potential for a kid to become engulfed in a omni-present secular culture is limitless.

And where are Mom and Dad?

You guessed it. They are absorbed with their own screens!

The 2018 Nielsen Audience Report found that adults are now spending more than 11 hours a day on media.[7] Add it up and adults will spend on the average 11 years of our lives involved with a cell phone ... 11 years in which we are not available to the children who are physically present in our lives. [7]

There is a word that describes our relationship to the screen.

That word is addiction.

TO SUMMARIZE

Today's kids are becoming screen disciples through secular venues like YouTube, Snapchat, Instagram and other media messaging. This strong secular-driven culture is ever-present in their lives, addictive and more readily available than Mom and Dad. It's where they go for advice, what to think, and how to behave. It's where they go for relationship and identity. Compare screen time with church time (1.7 times per month for an hour or two) and we have to admit: Our kids are screen disciples.

FAMILY BREAKDOWN

The second seismic shift affecting kids today has been the breakdown in family structure. For many Americans the intact, forever family is a fairy tale from a by-gone age.

Approximately 50% of American kids will witness the breakup of their parents' marriage. This fragmentation of the family has created a fatherless epidemic with more than 20 million American kids experiencing fatherless in the United States today. [8]

And what has family breakdown done to the values of a generation of kids? When Gen Z (anyone born after 1996) was polled and asked, "What matters?" they answered differently than Millennials or Gen Xers. A plurality of Gen Z said achievement matters, measured by financial success. Only one third of Gen Z said family mattered most as compared to Gen X and Millennials who put family first. Why we ask? When family is insecure a generation might look elsewhere for stability in life. The only way they might have a sense of belonging is through accomplishment. The only way they might feel secure is by having enough money. [9]

Why do we continue ministering to kids as if nothing has changed?

What does this mean?

It means family is no longer the primary influencer. Gen Z are disciples of and primarily influenced by their peers and by the screen.

How do we sync that reality with studies that have found parents are the primary influence in spiritual formation? [10] These findings have understandably driven KidMin programs to seek parental engagement as one of their pillars of programming. At Awana for nearly 70 years, parental involvement has been one of our foci as well. My husband, Steve and I wrote *Faith-Shaped Kids* to encourage parents to disciple their children, writing that "Children grow in the soil of their parents' faith." But there is a built-in assumption at work...that children have engaged and available parents in their lives. Unfortunately, the breakdown of the American family, including the national epidemic of fatherlessness and single mothering that is pervasive across all economic, social, and spiritual strati is the new norm.

Are we tone deaf to our surrounding culture and the realities of broken families sitting in our pews and living in our communities? Have we effectively trained and equipped parents to be able to disciple their own children and live up to our expectations of their place as primary in their children's' spiritual formation?

If today's child cannot be made disciples by their parents, **who then?**

TO SUMMARIZE

The church needs to stand in the gap as the belonging family and the primary influencers for a generation of kids whose parents are "missing" or unable to nurture them spiritually.

CHURCH DECLINE

Church closures are on the rise. Every week 100-200 churches close. That's 6,000 to 10,000 churches each year. [11]

But even more alarming is the answer to the question, "Are we losing our kids?" According to estimates from studies by the Barna Group the overall dropout rate in the past decade is 59 to 64%. This is a sobering measurement of the effectiveness of the discipleship of our kids. [12]

This often-cited data has led some to declare things like:

"We have lost a generation."

"The church is dying."

To fairly balance this alarming news, we need to look at other studies indicating that of those kids who leave the church in college, nearly two-third return and are currently attending church. [13]

There are already around four million resilient disciples out there.

But how many of this generation are disciples? Barna found that 10% of our kids between eighteen and twenty-nine met criteria for being resilient disciples. That's four million young people who are living a resilient, engaged faith. [14]

But what about the others? Are we doing the right things to retain them?

What is today's church kid's relationship to the church anyway? Some data shows that "church" children are attending church only 1.7 times a month. That equals 24 hours in church per year! [15] This is a stark contrast to the number of hours these kids are spending in front of their screens!

Kinnaman and Matlock made this conclusion in *Faith for Exiles* and we completely agree.

> *"The data indicates that an hour (or less) a week (in church)—or more likely, an hour or so every few weeks, when a young Christian shows up for church—is simply not a sufficient amount of "weight" to tone a heart bloated with hundreds of hours of content from digital Babylon (secular digital world input).* [16]

TO SUMMARIZE

The greatest challenge to the future of faith is the discipleship of our children.

What is the future of faith in America? Is the church on the way out, at least in western culture? And what about our kids who have opted out—when was the moment their feet stopped running in anticipation to church? When did they let go of our hands and stop wanting us "there?" What moment in time marked their identification with other tribes? When did their joy at belonging fade?

"

WILL WE REALIZE TOO LATE THAT
WE GAVE THEM THINGS THAT
DIDN'T TRAVEL INTO THEIR ADULT
LIVES AS ANYTHING MORE THAN
SPIRITUAL ENTERTAINMENT AND
MORALISTIC STORIES, THINGS
LACKING REAL SPIRITUAL POWER
AND PROACTIVE PURPOSE?"

WE HAVE FIERCE COMPETITION FOR THE SOULS OF THESE KIDS. ALL AROUND THE WORLD CHILDREN ARE BEING RECRUITED FOR RADICAL CAUSES—THE PASSIONS OF A "CROOKED AND TWISTED" GENERATION. THERE IS AN INTENSE BATTLE FOR THE HEART OF THE CHILD.

Years ago, shortly after I became CEO of Awana, two national Awana missionaries from Africa came to visit me.

"Do you know what the Muslims are doing in Africa?" they asked me. "They are building mosques and schools with oil money from the Middle East. Any child can get a free education. He or she just has to attend the mosque and then they can attend school gratis. They are going after the same children we are ministering to. What poor parent, even Christian, can walk away from the offer of free education for their children? That is how they are recruiting for the future. They are starting very young, with small children."

I am alarmed over this strategy that is working effectively, recruiting even Christian families to Islam.

We need our own global child discipleship strategy. We can start by recognizing these challenges to the future of faith—challenges to the family, challenges to the church and challenges brought on by an increasing secular media discipleship. If these challenges are a problem for us today, imagine if ignored, what enormous issues they will be in our kids' future. The year 2050 is closer than we think. We should hold our children close today, but we must also do everything we can to anticipate and to prepare him or her to let go of our hands and step into their futures as tomorrow's resilient disciples, fearless leaders of the church and influencers of the culture.

Today offers more than challenges. It offers opportunities ... opportunities to examine whether or not we are preparing today's kids to be the resilient remnant, the resilient disciples of tomorrow's church. Will they have the kind of spiritual strength that engages a culture with elasticity and flexibility?

Will they stand firm on biblical truth? Or will they break against the weight of culture? Will they be silenced and driven underground or blended into secular culture, Christians—but in name only?

It is time for an awakening of faith in America. We believe a renewal can start in the children's wing of the church. It can begin in your heart as you read this book.

Come together. There are mountains ahead of us. The church is struggling. Some say it is in decline or even dying. The family is breaking down. The screen is becoming a powerful disciple maker of our kids. Each of these mountains challenge the future of faith. But there is more. There is a threat that is beginning to show its face that is even more powerful, passionately anti-Christian and on the rise. It is an entire mountain range.

Words from Scripture resound in my spirit now, even as I write the above foreboding words. And it is these (John 16:33, NIV)

> "I have told you these things, so that in Me you may have peace. In this world you will have trouble. But take heart! I have overcome the world."

ESSENTIAL QUESTIONS:

Will our children always run to church?

What's the impact of a passive church in the midst of an active culture?

Is there hope for the future of the church?

Where do Christian families need to draw boundaries around a rising, highly-impactful secular culture?

THANK YOU BERNIE SANDERS... WAIT, WHAT?

CHAPTER 3

The 2016 election year was contentious.

Every day seemed to usher in some new cringe-producing assaults on civility. Divisiveness, name calling, meanness and outright lies ruled the day. After seeing the Broadway musical *Hamilton*, our family remarked that at least our nation's political differences weren't ending in duels. But still, we watched families and friendships become divided as previously genial people got sucked into the downward spiral of personal attack.

Christians weren't immune from these public exchanges of incivility. Many of us had some of our own "I-wish-I-could-take-that-back" moments. It was as if we were experiencing civility unraveling as part of our public entertainment.

And some of us enjoyed it.

Frederick Buechner described our attraction to anger this way: "Of the Seven Deadly Sins, anger is possibly the most fun. To lick your wounds, to smack your lips over grievances long past, to roll over your tongue the prospect of bitter confrontations still to come, to savor to the last toothsome morsel both the pain you are given and the pain you are giving back—in many ways it is a feast fit for a king. The chief drawback is that what you are wolfing down is yourself. The skeleton at the feast is you." [1]

But one lack-of-respect-for-other-people's viewpoints scenario was different from the rest. One public exchange informed the people of Christian faith about what we might expect in the future. We should pay very close attention to it. It wasn't front page headline news...but for those who caught it, a chill went down our collective people of faiths' spine. I encourage you to remove political bias from the following report. This is not meant as a political statement, or a suggestion about who to vote for, or who not to vote for, but rather a glimpse into the growing secular mindset about faith.

In June, 2016, during Senate confirmation hearings of President Trump nominee, Russell Vought (an evangelical Christian), Bernie Sanders completely ignored the No Religious Test Clause in the United States Constitution that separates church and state and limits government power over faith. Instead, Sanders focused on Vought's religious convictions.

Here is the transcript from that interview: Quoting Vought from an article he had written during a Wheaton College public debate on whether the God of the Old Testament was the same God as Allah, Sanders began with Vought's own words. [2]

Transcript
June 2016

Sanders: *"Muslims do not simply have a deficient theology. They do not know God because they have rejected Jesus Christ, His Son, and they stand condemned."*
He then asked Vought, *"Do you believe that that statement is Islamophobic?"*

Vought: *Absolutely not, Senator. I'm a Christian, and I believe in a Christian set of principles based on my faith. That post, as I stated in the questionnaire to this committee, was to defend my alma mater, Wheaton College, a Christian school that has a statement of faith that includes the centrality of Jesus Christ for salvation, and…*

Sanders *(Interrupting): I apologize. Forgive me, we just don't have a lot of time. Do you believe people in the Muslim religion stand condemned? Is that your view?*

Vought: *Again, Senator, I'm a Christian, and I wrote that piece in accordance with the statement of faith at Wheaton College.*

Sanders: *I understand that. I don't know how many Muslims there are in America. Maybe a couple million. Are you suggesting that all those people stand condemned? What about Jews? Do they stand condemned too?*

Vought: *Senator, I'm a Christian...*

Sanders: *I understand you are a Christian, but this country is made of people who are not just—I understand that Christianity is the majority religion, but there are other people of different religions in this country and around the world. In your judgment, do you think that people who are not Christians are going to be condemned?*

Vought: *Thank you for probing on that question. As a Christian, I believe that all individuals are made in the image of God and are worthy of dignity and respect regardless of their religious beliefs. I believe that as a Christian that's how I should treat all individuals...*

Sanders: *You think your statement that you put into that publication, they do not know God because they rejected Jesus Christ, His Son, and they stand condemned, do you think that's respectful of other religions?*

Vought: *Senator, I wrote a post based on being a Christian and attending a Christian school that has a statement of faith that speaks clearly in regard to the centrality of Jesus Christ in salvation.*

Sanders: *I would simply say, Mr. Chairman, that this nominee is really not someone who this country is supposed to be about.*[3]

3

"This nominee is really not someone who this country is supposed to be about!" [4] **Whoa!**

Let us be clear what Islamophobia means. According to Merriam-Webster, Islamophobia is an irrational fear of, aversion to, or discrimination against Islam or people who practice Islam. Other sources define it as hatred or fear of Muslims or of their politics or of their culture.

In that one public moment, Bernie Sanders gave Christian believers a shocking look at 2050. Emboldened and empowered, he linked traditional Christian belief to phobic hatred. In that one interview, he clearly attempted to marginalize timeless truth and minimalize the impact of Christian belief. This accusation is becoming familiar to us. The LGBT community accuses Christians of homophobia and hatred of homosexuals because orthodox Christianity rejects homosexual practice as normative and holds marriage to be a covenant between a man and a woman. In recent years to disagree with someone's position is to risk being accused of hatred.

But unfortunately, by 2050 the thought that "Christians are haters" may be commonly accepted. The backlash for believers from this societal direction is chilling.

It is time to prepare ourselves and our children to respond to those kinds of accusations, to insist on being fairly and accurately portrayed. Russell Vought was completely taken back by Bernie Sander's approach. Who wouldn't have been? But how differently that interview could have ended if Vought had answered, "Scripture says that God is not willing that any should perish. Nor am I. Scripture also says that believing in Jesus Christ is how we are saved. I believe the Bible along with millions of believers through the centuries."

BY 2050 THE THOUGHT THAT "CHRISTIANS ARE HATERS" MAY BE COMMONLY ACCEPTED.

Along these same lines the *Huffington Post* recently published a piece that was titled *Is the Church Dying?* This is a portion of that article:

1. First, if the Church wishes to have any kind of viable future, it must stop pretending the Bible is an infallible book written by God and dictated through Divinely-inspired and inerrant writers.

Frankly, I, for one, am so over this religious nonsense.

It's time religious people grow up and stop reading the Bible, if they read it at all, like it were a rule book dropped out of the sky by God herself.

2. Second, the Church will have to end its losing war with science, biology, and anthropology, if it expects to have any kind of reputable future.

You might not like what Darwin taught. But the only reason any Christian would not is because Darwin all but ruined our little creation myth in Genesis.

In fact, the Church is the laughingstock of the world when religious leaders seek to perpetuate the myth.

If you care at all about the future of the Church, you will have to update your theology. In other words, the old, old story does not work anymore.

3. Third, the church has lost its war against gender and race and sex and the discrimination it has waged in those contexts for decades.

Those days are over.

In fact, any institution, including the Church, that continues to perpetrate discrimination against people the institution may pretend to "love" but despises or resents overall, will disappear.

Is the Church Dying? The answer is an unequivocal "Yes." [5]

Why would a news source publish such a hostile and disrespectful perspective? Inflammatory writing increases readership apparently. But look a little deeper into the assumptions of this writer. His prescription for renewed church health overlooks that the majority of the 6,000 to 10,000 churches that are dying are mainline denominational churches. They are the very churches that followed this writer's preferred pathway for decades and now they are shutting their doors. It's a prescription for death.

Even though thousands of churches are closing their doors, there is a rebirth and growth of churches that are committed to Scripture and the exclusivity of Christ. One would think if this author was correct that these "old fashioned" churches would be dying. But the opposite is the case! The fastest growing churches aren't the ones that are progressive. They are the ones that have stood faithful. [6]

It's really not hard to imagine that, tomorrow, the attitude of America about religion will undoubtedly be similar to the *Huffington Post* writer ...

- *shockingly superior,*
- *publicly scornful and*
- *totally dismissive of orthodox evangelical Christianity.*

These children we love will be the church of 2050. They will need to be disciples as few modern generations before them have had to be. They will need to have spine and heart—spine to stand firm for Christian beliefs in an increasingly hostile secular world, spine to insist on being fairly characterized and heart to embrace that same intolerant-of-faith world with a love that can't be ignored.

If all the challenges facing this generation of adults-to-be are mountains ...

- *the breakdown of the family,*
- *the secular discipleship of their generations through a heightened velocity of internet influence and*
- *the decline of the Church.*

Then ...

the post-Christian thought that challenges Christian beliefs with public anti-Christian attacks is an entire mountain range.

Looming over the future, aimed full-force at our children as they come into their adulthoods is a belief system that declares Christian thought to no longer be an acceptable part of the cultural dialogue. By then public consensus may decide that we, the church, are "not the people this country should be about."

Our kids. Will they stand firm? Will they proudly proclaim their faith? Will they go about God's work in the world fearlessly and bravely, unashamed of who they are and what they believe? Will the gospel be their clear loyalty? Will they be resilient?

If the answer is "Yes!" then they will faithfully join those who have followed Christ for centuries.

Let me remind those who want to silence Christian thought, what we, who this country shouldn't be about, contribute to the world and why our voice, though contrarian, is important.

We are generous givers.

In 2013, *The Chronicle of Philanthropy* reported that giving by evangelicals outpaced secular giving. [6] In 2017, a report by the ECFA (Evangelical Council for Financial Accountability) stated that the giving of evangelicals that year was 16.2 billion and growing annually. [7]

This charitable giving is remarkable. But why isn't the secular culture seeing us through that lens?

Where does our money go?

"

THESE CHILDREN WE LOVE WILL BE
THE CHURCH OF 2050. THEY WILL
NEED TO BE DISCIPLES AS FEW
MODERN GENERATIONS BEFORE
THEM HAVE HAD TO BE. THEY
WILL NEED TO HAVE SPINE AND
HEART—SPINE TO STAND FIRM
FOR CHRISTIAN BELIEFS IN AN
INCREASINGLY HOSTILE SECULAR
WORLD AND HEART TO EMBRACE
THAT SAME INTOLERANT-OF-FAITH
WORLD WITH A LOVE THAT CAN'T
BE IGNORED."

Behind many church walls are care centers that provide for the poorest of the poor in their communities. Every church is acquainted with needy people who come for help with food, employment and housing. That happens wherever there is a Christian church. No one asks, "Are you gay, Muslim or Jewish?" No one in need is excluded from compassionate care.

The church has dug wells and rescued sexually exploited women and children. We have built schools, hospitals and clinics. We have responded to poverty by pulling children out of dead-end lives, educating them and giving them futures. Because believers were willing to write a check every month to sponsor a child's progress through life, we have reversed the downward trajectory of poverty in many countries of the world. We have held the dying, comforted the sick and loved the orphaned.

Sometimes we have been martyred and hated for this work in the world.

Still we go on because ...

We believe people are made in the image of God and deserve to be treated with dignity.

For centuries, Christ and His followers have had a world-shaping impact. How easy it is to assume the goodness Jesus ushered into the world was always here. We forget what true paganism was like, though we are getting glimpses of its return today. Jesus looked in our faces and saw our dignity— that we were made in the image of God. "He dined with the outcasts, touched the unclean, recruited women into his ministry, and chased hypocrites." [8]

Children and women were lifted from property status to human status because of Jesus. His influence civilized the pagan world. He introduced us to forgiveness, humility, treatment of enemies, respect of women and children.

When the church lived out the truth of the gospel in their daily lives, the pre-Christian world was introduced to God's design for human flourishing, lived in a way they had never seen before.

Those values of Jesus have been embraced by all races, classes and sexes for thousands of years. It became the ideal that permeated the hopes of constitutions, governments and this world ever since.

This world cannot afford to not be about Christianity!

> "Christianity matters. It is the very core and center of Western civilization. Many of the best things about our world are the result of Christianity, and some of the worst things are the result of its absence, or moving away from it." [9]

I wonder, then, who ever told Bernie Sanders that we were haters?

Maybe we did.

In the heat of our current political debates perhaps we have forgotten the plan, the strategy for living Christianly in a hostile world. What would our social media feeds indicate about us this year? Did our political passions outrun our Christian passions?

Did our political passions outrun our Christian passions?

> "Put to death whatever belongs to your earthly nature... You used to walk in these ways in the life you once lived. But now you must rid yourselves of all such things as these: anger, rage, malice, slander and filthy language from your lips...Therefore as God's chosen people...clothe ourselves with compassion, kindness, humility, gentleness and patience." [10]

Colossians 3:5-9

Clothe yourselves means to be disciplined in our public interactions. It is the part of ourselves that people see, that they interact with, that they know. Those public selves and those social media selves need to be Christlike.

At Awana, we are calling this public stance in the world Spine and Heart. We know today's children in 2050 will need high capacity to live publicly Christian—they will need Spine to live unapologetically Christian and to expect respect for their beliefs and Heart to love those in a culture who differ or stand opposed to them.

The church needs to commit itself to Resilient Child Discipleship if we hope to face the future with a resilient remnant of resistant and loving disciples.

Resilient Child Discipleship

The process of a Christ-follower committing meaningful, intentional, and consistent time and space to a child or a group of children so that they may know who Jesus is and are known by a body of believers (Belong), to place their faith in Jesus and apply the Word of God (Believe), and to reproduce their own discipleship (Become) so that a third spiritual generation can lead and love like Jesus Christ.

Just as miners took a canary down into the mines, to ensure there was still enough air, because without air, the canary would die first, the church's "canary," its most symptomatic indicator of health, is our younger generations.

The canary is not dead. And though there are many challenges, God is still working. All that is missing is for the church to be the Church ... the mature bride of Christ, steadfast and abounding in love.

We are radical lovers.

When I read how the early church in the Roman era rescued babies from death by exposure, I am reminded of one of the most beautiful characteristics of the church. Every week we see it in the "seek and save" rescue hand that is extended into the church's surrounding communities, especially the hand that rescues children whose lives are already beyond human help.

Jamie was just such a child. He grew up in his grandmother's home, just the two of them. The summer between third and fourth grade "Granny," a victim of Alzheimers, left their home one night. By the grace of God, a police officer found her and brought her home. But the next morning, Jamie's young world was turned upside down. A woman from the Department of Family Services came by the house and said that a 9-year-old could not be the primary caregiver to an elderly woman with Alzheimers. Jamie's Granny was taken away in an ambulance and Jamie was taken to his cousin's house. That was the last time Jamie saw his grandmother.

During this time, Jamie was a guest of a friend who needed to bring someone to club to pass a section in his Awana handbook. The assignment was to "Invite a Friend." Jamie was that friend. Every week he was picked up by a bus and driven to club. And while that bus was making its stops headed for the church, the bus driver and his wife ministered to Jamie. They told him that God loved him and that there was a place called church where he belonged. Every week he learned verses, and found friends. Soon he trusted Jesus as his Savior and developed a passion for serving. As a bus kid himself, he has a love for those who find themselves without that important at-home Christian influence.

PICTURED: *Jamie and Donna Root with Daughter Shannon*

Today Jamie serves Awana as a full-time field missionary in the U.S. Jamie is not only a resilient disciple, but also a resilient disciple maker.

His life speaks to the power of the church when it loves. With no parents on board in his life, the church became the place where his need for belonging and believing translated into becoming.

In our spiritual DNA the church is loaded with thousands of years of healing. We already know how to lead our divided country into a place of healing. For broken children or a broken nation the hope is found in the way of Jesus, a pathway that God's people have been traveling for thousands of years. We know how to love radically and when we do...everything can change. Including the future.

So thank you Bernie Sanders for giving us a glimpse of the future. The year 2050 is coming. Likely, he and I will be gone, but before then, you and I will do everything to insure that our children will be ready.

ESSENTIAL QUESTIONS:

How has recent culture changed toward Christians?

What are the 2050 problems in the making?

Are we preparing ourselves and the next generations to stand firm, even with our faith on trial?

RADICAL LOVE COULD HAVE SAVED NIKOLAS CRUZ—

the Parkland Shooter

CHAPTER 4

It was February 17, 2018—three days after America experienced the most tragic school shooting in our history.

Parkland, Florida, had just lost 17 of their children. And now, two days later, I found myself being interviewed by a Christian radio program broadcasting in South Florida, including Parkland where the shootings had taken place.

I don't remember what the radio host asked me. I just remember feeling brokenhearted and compelled to speak of something beyond the ceaseless, as-yet-unresolvable debate on gun control or the probable causes for someone to behave so ruthlessly that are the usual and typical media covering of school shootings. I found myself reaching into my heart to search for some word of hope, some insight that would comfort, something that could shed some light and possibly stop the carnage. Where were the words that God lived in ... the engodded perspective that would shed His light on our national tragedy?

Without premeditation I suddenly found myself saying, "Radical love could have saved Nikolas Cruz—the Parkland Shooter." Even as I said it, I realized it might sound like a simple over statement to many people, including some Christ followers. Could radical love have broken through to a disturbed 19-year-old who was gun-obsessed and angry enough to kill 17 kids his age and wound 17 others? Could radical love have performed an early intervention and walked through his life challenges with him so he was not alone? Could radical love have changed the trajectory of this tragic story and life?

COULD RADICAL LOVE HAVE CHANGED THE TRAJECTORY OF THIS TRAGIC STORY AND LIFE?

In the days that followed, other radio outlets and print media picked up my remarks. "Radical Love Could Have Saved Nikolas Cruz," was their lead in. When I heard that phrase with my name attached, I repeatedly asked myself, "Do I really believe that?"

Each time my conviction grew stronger and my heart echoed back, "Yes! I believe it!" Radical love could have saved the Parkland shooter from targeting his pain and suffering into the world until 17 innocent classmates lay dead at his feet.

The national debate on gun control is a stuck needle and impotent. Looking to our government for hope or solutions that will protect our children is already too little too late. Mental health experts weigh in, but in the end, nothing much seems to be reversing this cycle of violence. Debate falls short. But even as the news of radicalized-by-hatred students rampaging through their campuses seems to be a nightmare we can't wake up from, we cannot give up hope.

IT STARTS WITH KIDS. REALLY. WHEN WE LOVE A COMMUNITY'S CHILDREN, WE WILL HAVE MORE INFLUENCE AND MORE CHURCH GROWTH THAN WE CAN HANDLE

The hope for our culture is found in the way of Jesus—the living out of the redemptive work of the gospel. But ... and this is a huge but, **we must remember how to love radically.**

"Well, what does radical love look like in our churches today?" the radio interviewer asked me.

"It starts with kids. Really. When we love a community's children, we will have more influence and more church growth than we can handle. We may also heal a child who is on his or her way to pumping the world with his or her pain from the trigger of an AR-15 assault rifle. Radical love is salvation, redemption, repurpose, redirection, accompaniment and championing. It is the beauty of the gospel alive through the church."

Radical Love Opens Doors

Radical love is the kind that opens a church's door to every child within its reach. That means the kid with behavior problems, children from dysfunctional and hard-to-work-with homes, the children of poverty, children who are already social outcasts, children with special needs, children of different nationalities and tongues. The others. The different. The quirky. The odd. The left out. The overlooked. The abused. The neglected. The hungry. The lonely. The bullied. The ones already sliding into despair. The exploited. The trafficked. The immigrant. When Jesus said, "Let the children come," I'm pretty sure He wasn't thinking about only church kids whose lives are supported by believing, loving homes. His words were also meant to carry those "other" kids through our church doors and into our hearts."

Our legitimate concerns with retention studies that indicate we are losing our own kids has focused on only one part of the child world … "our" kids. But what about the others?

When a church throws open its doors and "lets the children come," it changes everything. I'm touched by the kind of love these "let-the-children-come" churches give to kids.

Radical love looks a lot like Oakwood Baptist Church in New Braunfels, Texas. This church started Awana only recently. Not long after I ran into their Senior Pastor, Ray Still, and their Executive Pastor, Rusty Rice. These two pastors were eager to tell me what their first year partnering with Awana had been like.

"We thought we might have 100 kids come, but instead a couple hundred more are showing up." This "abundance of children" forced them to make some choices … go normal, or go radical. Should they cut off the number of kids who were allowed to come? Should they restrict it to their own church kids? Sadly, that is often the difficult decision churches are forced to make. But no, they didn't "go normal." They didn't "go easy."

They went radical. It meant finding twice the number of adults to help out. Everyone on paid staff from the pastors and down through the ranks had to show up to register kids, lead small groups, organize game time, listen to verses, and lead the large group times.

"

WHEN JESUS SAID, "LET THE CHILDREN COME," I'M PRETTY SURE HE WASN'T THINKING ABOUT ONLY CHURCH KIDS WHOSE LIVES ARE SUPPORTED BY BELIEVING, LOVING HOMES. HIS WORDS WERE MEANT TO CARRY THOSE "OTHER" KIDS THROUGH OUR CHURCH DOORS AND INTO OUR HEARTS."

But these men were smiling as they told me about their situation. They were excited to share the news of their abundance of children with me.

"Yes, we all showed up. It was crazy. But it was also exciting. So we decided, why not? Let's go all out and feed them all pizza on Awana night."

Formula for radical-crazy-kid love right there! I thought to myself.

But there was more. Pastor Ray wanted to talk about a special kid in his small group of nine grade school boys.

"I have this one kid in my group who is a nightmare," he said, still smiling. "He is a full-time job for me almost every week. Recently, I met his mother. I said 'I would like to talk to you about your son.

"I saw her face drop as she prepared herself for the familiar-to-her bad news."

He continued "I told her, we love having your boy at our church. He is always welcome here and we are doing just great."

Ray paused to let his emotions pass. "I saw her face light up. She had steeled herself for the usual bad report. I could see how surprised she was that finally there was a word of encouragement coming from somewhere in the world about her child!"

A couple of hours a week in the presence of caring adults who show God's radical love in their community to each and every child can change everything. Even chance encounters can carry the power to change lives.

Here's to the radical love of a pastor who gets out of the pulpit once a week to sit at a kid-sized table to love and disciple kids from his community!

I know this may sound radical to our Awana community, but Wess Stafford, President Emeritus of Compassion International and a current Awana board member, explained it this way, "Sometimes the most important thing that could fill in the blanks of a child's handbook is not that they have successfully memorized Scripture that week, but something that says, "You are a great kid. God loves you and we are so glad you're here!"

That's what radical love looks like. It's not something you get from having the "right" curriculum or program. It's a heart for God that puts kids first. **"We are loved into loving Jesus."**[1]

Who knows what each of us is capable of without the redeeming work of God in our lives? We are saved from our sin and we are saved from what we might have become. Of all people, we know the power of God unto salvation, the reality of changed and freed lives, and the impact of radical love.

But there was a church.

When the current leadership team at Awana was forming, we decided to share our childhood stories with each other. One by one, the childhood pain unfolded as we trusted each other with our most vulnerable selves. We were a "broken early" group. One remembered the night his father rampaged through their home, packing to leave his family forever ... all while his older brother shielded him with his body, reading a book out loud to distract him from the adult potentially-violent scene that was unfolding. Another shared how he was beaten by his mother every morning before school for wetting his bed as a child. She waited until everyone else had left for the morning then, when they were home alone together, she would beat him. Every morning. No one knew the shameful secret of his mother's behavior that he bore in his childhood body. A writer shared what he had written for his father's funeral, a man who was a Vietnam veteran, and an angry, abusive father. I wondered as we listened, *how do you sum up the life of a man who broke you as a child? Do you still call him "father?"*

One after another the painful truths were told. We shared our brokenness. We took off our masks that made us appear beautiful and untouched and showed each other our scars. We shared what was done to us behind closed doors. We grieved that those who should have loved us rejected us and left us with the imprint of adult sin on our lives. We grieved for each other.

But we shared more than our brokenness. Interestingly, a pattern of another kind was emerging from our stories. We all shared something else in common. All of our stories ended with the phrase, **"But, there was a church ... "**

"I was my mother's whipping boy, but there was a church who loved me."

"No one knew how dysfunctional we were and how abused and humiliated I was at home, but there was a church where people fathered and mothered me."

"My dad abandoned my mother and me, he just walked out of our lives, but there was a church who took my mom and me to its heart."

We all had "knowing" pasts. But we had more. In all of our lives, there was a church that made all the difference. And in that sacred place, we had found radical love. We belonged!

That's why we believe without reservation that faithful churches can love in a way that can make all the difference for the Nikolas Cruzes and all the "us too" children—like we were—of this world.

We never know how desperate a child's need might be or what they might be experiencing at adult hands, or why that child has come into our lives, or into our church at this time. But we can be sure of this. If they are there, God is doing a work in their lives and we are a part of their story. Maybe they will lead an international discipleship ministry to children when they grow up. Maybe God will use their knowing pasts.

When I'm working on the West Coast, I occasionally attend Calvary Church in Westlake Village, California where my friend, Shawn Thornton, pastors. This is a beautiful and affluent church set in the coastal hills. One Sunday I made a surprise visit and thought that afterwards I would stand in line to say "Hi!" and greet Shawn. I had a long, but interesting wait. How can I say this? The people who reached Shawn ahead of me were children with disabilities, adults in wheelchairs and others who struggled to speak clearly or express their thoughts. I smiled as I realized that as successful a pastor as Shawn is, these are his special people.

The pieces of who Shawn is came together for me that morning. I had read his book about his childhood called *All But Normal*. He described life at home with a mother who was suffering from TBI—Traumatic Brain Injury and the trauma of living with a mother who is often in fits of rage and dangerous. She also taught Sunday school and was an Awana leader. One night was particularly etched in his memory:

"It had been a night of hell like no other in our house.

'I'm tired of this! I'm not living like this anymore! I'm going to divorce you," Mom shrieked.

"Go ahead," Dad yelled back. "What do I care?"

"Most of these battles died out after a little while, but 30 minutes later this one was still going strong.

From across the room, Mom grabbed something and threw it at Dad, hitting the cabinets near his head. In anger Dad whirled around and threw something back at her, not full force but enough to warn her not to do it again."

"Boys, go to your rooms," Dad said.

Troy and I didn't hesitate. We wanted out of there as much as they wanted us gone.

The raging went on for hours, walls pummeled with unseen objects, accusations of the most penetrating kind wielded like daggers.

I heard the front door open, and out my window I saw something that wrenched my heart apart: my mother, her body so stiff she could barely walk, breath coming in angry huffs.

PICTURED: *Shawn as a child*

It was the night my mother was taken to the mental ward." [1]

But no one at church realized the trouble they were in at home. Still, church was the safe place. And today, Shawn is a pastor with a "knowing" past. It's why every Sunday Shawn stands and receives the stories and comments from anyone who needs a piece of his time. It's why he does it week after week. It's how God uses his "knowing" past.

He explains it like this: "Before taking the pulpits on Sundays, I often found myself imagining who was sitting in the congregation that day and what they were struggling with. I visualized wealthy people who had family members held captive by alcohol or drugs. I pictured poor people who had just heard they had cancer and had no way of paying for treatment. I thought of grandparents whose grandkids didn't visit anymore, men who had lost their jobs, kids who were lonely. Hundreds of scenarios played through my head, and I felt the pain of each of them.

NO MATTER HOW BAD OR BROKEN LIFE SEEMED, GOD MET US WITH HOPE.

I realized our family possessed something in our little house on Victory Road that many people simply didn't have: the love and the purpose of God in the midst of seeming chaos. No matter how bad or broken life seemed, God met us with hope. The insight this gave me into people's lives was almost a sixth sense ... somehow in the context of craziness and pain, God had given me a pastor's heart." [2]

A sixth sense. That's radical love born of a knowing past.

We may never know their whole stories.

But this we know. We are the church. His body. His light in an increasingly dark world.

We have, not only the advantage of a knowing past, but we have a way to love with a radical love that belongs to Christ-followers alone.

It starts with children, even if we are tempted to believe it starts with Washington, D.C.

Albert Mohler, President of Southern Baptist Theological Seminary, asks some hard questions when it comes to the kind of love the church is offering kids today:

> Beyond the question of birth rates, what are we (not) doing with the kids we have? I think the answer to that is direct and straightforward. We have surrendered Sunday school and youth ministry in many of our churches. I am the product of being involved in the local church many hours a week as a boy and teenager. My frame of reality was largely set by my parents' design—and it was church whenever the church offered an opportunity, and there were many opportunities: Sunday school, youth choir, Royal Ambassadors (for boys) and Acteens (for girls). There were weekly youth fellowships and youth meetings and regular retreats. There were wonderful and faithful adult volunteers, as well as a faithful youth minister. Christian Smith and his research associates found that one of the distinguishing marks of young people who continue in their church participation as adults was that they had developed a warm and trusting relationship with an adult in the church (even **just one**) other than their own parents. [3]

Radical love was once normative for the church, but today radical love is too often the exception. Radical love goes beyond what's expected to a whole life-defining way of relating to a generation of kids. It's so much more than volunteering.

Radical love might move you beyond volunteerism and cause you to become a child champion: You speak up for the value of children in your church. You raise the bar for the importance of volunteering that is faithful, dependable and passionate for kids.

Radical love might move you beyond child championing to becoming a generational guardian—someone who is there for kids through their childhoods, their young adulthoods and at every step of their journey. You walk the walk throughout your lifetimes together.

Radical love might make you the "kid-friendliest" church in town. You might end up with everyone's kids. You are kid-challenged and kid-challenging. You are the ones who can make the greatest investment and difference. Yes!

In our organization, when we ask churches in their exit polls "Why are you leaving?" more than anything else they say, "Not enough volunteers." "We are moving everything to one hour on Sunday." "We need something that is easier."

Sad. I wonder if we have made this more complicated than it should be. That's our part in this failure of sorts. At a time when the church needs to be exerting greater effort into ensuring the future of faith by discipling kids, some have become discouraged, given up or have grown apathetic about their own futures and their children's futures. I check my heart. Yes, I believe radical love could have saved Nikolas Cruz.

And I believe something else as well.

Radical love could be the fearless future of faith, if we just remember how.

ESSENTIAL QUESTIONS:

Do you believe radical church love could be the solution to our country's epidemic of gun violence. Why or why not?

List the ways the church could extend radical love to a community.

To whom does the church need to extend radical love? What people groups do we need to love more radically as Jesus Himself would? What groups think they are beyond Christian love?

How can we examine our hearts, make adjustments and change our culture's perception about the limits of Jesus' love?

FIRE CARRIERS

CHAPTER 5

In Cormac McCarthy's novel, *No Country for Old Men*, Sheriff Bell remembers that his father would carry the embers from the campfire in one camp to the next in an animal horn.

It was a tradition passed to the cowboys from the Native American Indians. [1]

The fire carrier was important to western life.

> *The fire carrier brought hope ... fire chased the darkness from the western skies. The night was not so ominous when a fire was burning.*
>
> *The fire carrier helped continue the mission ... hunters could keep hunting, continuing their search far from home. Cowboys could continue protecting their herds from predators.*
>
> *The fire carrier sustained life ... food could be cooked and made edible and become life giving.*

So too, today, stories—the fires we carry to each other—hold a special place in our lives. In the lines of a story, we can find healing, life and light for our journeys.

And so was such a story. It began very simply, but it lit up the earth for thousands of years with its hopeful truth. It transformed everything. The fire it carried still burns brightly today. This is that story's opening line:

In the beginning, God created the heavens and the earth.

That was fire!

In a pagan, wildly senseless, brutally hopeless world that story carried fire.

It meant we weren't random beings. We were wanted, created and pursued by God. Here was meaning.

The story continued. Man turned away, but God didn't extinguish the flame and give us over to darkness. Just the opposite. He called us His children, not just His creations. He loved us and still we turned our faces from Him. Over and over that pattern repeated.

But then a new part of the story lit up the world.

> *In the beginning was the Word, and the Word was with God, and the Word was God. He was with God in the beginning. Through Him all things were made; without Him nothing was made that has been made. In Him was life, and that life was the light of all. The light shines in the darkness and the darkness has not overcome it. (John 1:1-5)*

And with those beginning words to his Gospel, John carried fire to the world.

The light shines in the darkness, and the darkness has not overcome it!

We can barely imagine how those words pierced the pagan heart with hope. The disciples and the apostles of the early church carried that fire to Jerusalem, Judea and Samaria. For centuries, mothers and fathers of all skin colors and nationalities have gathered their children around their knees and breathed the fire of God's love into their children's' hearts with that same story. Preachers have carried that fire in their sermons. Missionaries have carried that story to the ends of the earth.

But the fire was often resisted. The story attacked. Ancient Rome tried to silence the fire-carrying story of Jesus' death, burial and resurrection. They persecuted the fire carriers and put them to death by crucifixion, stoning, the sword and flames. Christian tradition holds that all the disciples of Jesus, save John, died martyrs' deaths. Early Christian fire carriers were torn to pieces by wild animals to the roar of bloodthirsty crowds, but all the power and terror of ancient Rome could not put out that fire. The story of God's love still burns brightly today and ancient Rome is only a crumbling ruin of what once was. The Jesus story turned the world upside down.

Nazi Germany tried to silence the story of Jesus. Fire carriers like Dietrich Bonhoeffer and thousands of other Christian leaders died in Nazi concentration camps. Executed by death squads, gassed, starved, and worked to death, still the evil darkness of Nazi Germany could not put out the Christian fire. Today, God's love burns brightly, but Nazi Germany is defeated, relegated to a shameful, repugnant chapter of human history.

> *In Him was life, and that life was the light of all.*
>
> *The light shines in the darkness, and the darkness has not overcome it. (John 1:4-5)*

In my childhood, the Russians were always coming. Children of my generation were taught to "duck and cover" under our desks for air raid drills. Russia, with its enforced secular anti-God, state-is-everything, death pogroms of Stalin and others were a force of darkness sweeping the world. Christian fire carriers were driven underground and subjected to state terror. But today, the Berlin wall is torn down and Russia is no longer the threat it once was.

> *In Him was life, and that life was the light of all men.*
>
> *The light shines in the darkness and the darkness has not overcome it. (John 1:4-5)*

At so many points in world history the fire could have been extinguished, the story buried and forgotten. But generation after generation of fire carriers kept the gospel ember burning. Fire carriers like Peter and Paul, John and Stephen, St Augustine, St. Patrick, George Whitefield, John Wesley, D.L. Moody, William Carey, Amy Carmichael and Billy Graham carried the ember of the gospel story that continues to light up the world.

AT SO MANY POINTS IN WORLD HISTORY THE FIRE COULD HAVE BEEN EXTINGUISHED, THE STORY BURIED AND FORGOTTEN. BUT GENERATION AFTER GENERATION OF FIRE CARRIERS KEPT THE GOSPEL EMBER BURNING.

But these fire carriers were not alone. Though their individual embers burned brightly, they were easily snuffed out. But there was a church. The church fanned the flames of the fire carriers and carried the embers to the entire world. The church, those Christ-followers with spine and heart, refused to be silenced, refused to be driven underground, refused to stop carrying the fire. At great risk and sacrifice the church spoke truth into their generations and were God's love to the world.

That is the world's most awesome story. It's still the fire that lights up the world. It's the story whose flames we protect and stoke today. The church, led by fire carriers of our generation, must proclaim God's truth and love. We must proclaim it peacefully, persistently, clearly, fearlessly and with boldness. We must proclaim it so it lights a fire in our world.

Why? Because ...

> *In Him was life, and that life was the light of all men.*
>
> *The light shines in the darkness, and the darkness has not overcome it.*
> *(John 1:4-5)*

We can face the future fearlessly. God is writing this story. And it is still fire.

In my neighborhood, we have an email chain where local neighbors can post information or ask each other for help to find plumbers, remove skunks, locate lost cats and dogs, warn each other about mice sightings in local restaurants or advertise for upcoming garage sales.

It's all very Americana and quite charming in a neighborly kind of way.

It's also a good feel for the pulse of what's happening in the arena of public opinion. I am not a very active member, but recently a conversation took a direction I knew I needed to join. I confess, I wanted to avoid it, but a convicting voice spoke to me saying, "How can you expect to teach others, especially children, to have spine and heart if you avoid these kinds of conversations yourself?"

This is how it began:

NEIGHBOR 1

Does anyone know what the crowd is about downtown?

NEIGHBOR 2

They are protesting abortion.

👍 2

NEIGHBOR 3

It's their right to assemble and protest of course. But I really wish they didn't include their kids in these demonstrations. Child labor laws? Should be against the law to force young kids to further a specific agenda, no matter what it is.

👍 10

NEIGHBOR 4

I agree.

👍 3

BOOM! This is what happened next:

NEIGHBOR 5

I hope everyone who thinks this should be against child labor laws is also against children marching for gay pride, gender equality and so on, just sayin …

👍 15

Why were these 15 people, including me, so silent up until now? I finally decided to join in, but only after Neighbor Five led the way:

MY RESPONSE

> *Your protection of children in regards to child labor laws seems ironic. Wouldn't children be better protected if we extended this care to their very lives?*

👍 15

NEIGHBOR 6

> *There is a great deal of irony. Most of them are hypocrites. No sign saying, "Let me adopt or help pay for your child or abortion."*

👍 5

NEIGHBOR 7

> *Wish they would keep their religion and their politics to themselves. On this type of platform, your religion should be kept to yourself. Your religious opinions should be silenced.*

👍 10

Whoa! The assumptions made by this original post (that all her neighbors agreed with her right to choose perspective) made me weigh in. Many of us were silently disagreeing.

But what really caught my attention was the comment that religious opinions should be silenced. Silenced! That received 10 likes! I heard shades of Bernie Sanders in that "they should be silenced" comment. It sounded similar in thought to, "This nominee is really not someone this country is supposed to be about." The tide of public opinion against Christian thought is rising, even in our friendly little neighborhoods.

Spine and Heart

Looking back, I'm glad I went public. It encouraged others to speak out as well. But I also think I could have done a little better. I had more spine than heart. I could have agreed that the pictures of aborted babies were too graphic for most children, especially those caught unaware driving by in a car without any warning or explanation. Just BANG! and suddenly they are subjected to those pictures. I think my neighbors had a point in objecting to children being so exposed.

I wish I had said something like this. "Yes, the pictures are huge, graphic and maybe too much for kids. But while your concern for children is admirable, I find it ironic that your concern doesn't seem to extend to their very lives."

That would have been a better response. Spine AND Heart. Spine points to truth. Heart builds a bridge that wins that truth favor. It validates someone else's perspective, while still disagreeing. Our engagement with the world needs to include both.

Spine engagement by itself is too often argumentative, offensive and repulsive. Just read through Facebook to get tons of examples of this. Spine has to be served with plenty of heart to be heard and effective.

I've often wondered if Russell Vought might have answered Bernie Sanders differently had Russell put his answers through a spine and heart criteria.

For example when Bernie Sanders asked, (referring to a piece that Vought wrote) "Muslims do not simply have a deficient theology. They do not know God because they have rejected Jesus Christ, His Son, and they stand condemned." He then asked Vought, "Do you believe that that statement is Islamaphobic?"

Russell's answer? "Absolutely not, Senator. I'm a Christian and I believe in a Christian set of principles based on my faith."

Spine there, I'd say, truth and principles.

Sanders, interrupting, "Forgive me, we just don't have a lot of time. Do you believe people in the Muslim religion stand condemned? Is that your view?"

Vought answers, "Senator, I'm a Christian."

Spine again. After several similar exchanges, Sanders makes his final pronouncement. "I would simply say, Mr. Chairman, that this nominee is really not someone this country is supposed to be about."

Maybe things might have gone differently if Vaughn had answered like this: "Senator, Scripture says that God is not willing that any should perish. The message of Christianity is a message of love, not exclusivity. God is not willing that any should perish. Whether or not to respond to that love is each person's choice. But God desires that no one would be condemned. That is my desire and orthodox Christianity's desire as well."

Spine and Heart

Here is the catch: if our Christian "set of principles" focuses with greater volume and velocity on side principles, if our public dialogue is caught up in current issues only, if it is only capital letter SPINE, it's possible the main story will be overshadowed by side issues.

When we speak Christian values into current issues— gender identity, sexual preferences, abortion—we must be careful not to fall into the trap laid for us. We should have spine and refuse as well as object to arguments against us that label us "haters" because we don't accept

> **THE MESSAGE OF CHRISTIANITY IS A MESSAGE OF LOVE, NOT EXCLUSIVITY. GOD IS NOT WILLING THAT ANY SHOULD PERISH.**

or celebrate choices that are being made. But we must, additionally, be sure that our attitudes and actions are those that reflect the main story of God's love, sacrifice and redemption for humankind (heart). That is how we can carry the fire of God's love to our culture today.

The resilient church needs to engage our secular culture with spine, redefining truth and refusing to accept false interpretations of who we are, and heart, loving in word and deed. We especially need to teach this way of engaging our secular post-Christian culture to our children. The year 2050 will require a different way of keeping the flame of Christianity burning. It will be against the tide of public opinion. There will be effort to "silence" it. But unless we all want to live in a world without moral consciousness, we need to continue speaking up.

Tertullian, an early church apologist (160 – 220) imagined the best defense of faith being a good offense. He believed that Christian life as taught in Scripture and practiced in the church was morally superior. He imagined pagans looking at Christians and saying, "Look how they love each other ... for they themselves (pagans) hate one another; and how (Christians) are ready to die for each other (for pagans are ready to kill each other). [2]

What if we were more loving than argumentative? What if when we opened our mouths the love of God came rushing forth? What if the post-Christian secular world saw how we loved each other and how we loved them?

That would be fire!

WHAT IF WHEN WE OPENED OUR MOUTHS THE LOVE OF GOD CAME RUSHING FORTH?

A friend posted this on Facebook recently. I loved the way it describes social kindness:

Small Kindnesses

I've been thinking about the way, when you walk down a crowded aisle, people pull up their legs to let you by. Or how strangers still say, "Bless you!" when someone sneezes, a leftover from the Bubonic plague.

"Don't die," we are saying.

And sometimes when you spill lemons from your grocery bag, someone else will help you pick them up. Mostly, we don't want to harm each other. We want to be handed our cup of coffee hot, and to say, "Thank you!" to the person handing it. To smile at them and for them to smile back. For the waitress to call us honey when she sets down the bowl of clam chowder, and for the driver in the red pickup truck to let us pass.

We have so little for each other now. So far from fire and tribe. Only these brief moments of exchange. What if they are the true dwelling of the holy, these fleeting temples we make together when we say, "Here, have my seat." "Go ahead—you first." "I like your hat."[3]

So far from fire and tribe indeed! So far from "See how they love each other."

I take comfort from Matthew 16:18 and how these words of Jesus to Peter have played out down through the centuries and the fearless hope it gives me about the church in the year 2050.

> *Upon this rock, I will build My church, and the gates of hell shall not prevail against it.*

What does this mean for us today?

> *Upon this rock, I will build My church, and the gates of* secular opinion; social media, journalism, political correctness and media *shall not prevail against it.*

> *Upon this rock, I will build My church, and the gates of* higher education, the arrogant intellectualization of man's truth that disregards God's truth *shall not prevail against it.*

> *Upon this rock, I will build My church, and the gates of* government; the laws ignoring conscience and religious freedom *shall not prevail against it.*

> *Upon this rock, I will build My church, and the gates of* scientific theory, evolution, and quantum physics *shall not prevail against it.*

> *Upon this rock, I will build My church, and the gates of* technological secularism, the values and influence of the screen *shall not prevail against it.*

> *Upon this rock, I will build My church, and the gates of* family breakdown, divorce and fatherlessness *shall not prevail against it.*

> *Upon this rock, I will build My church, and the gates of* church lethargy *shall not prevail against it.*

"

THE CHURCH FANNED THE
FLAMES OF THE FIRE CARRIERS
AND CARRIED THE EMBERS TO
THE ENTIRE WORLD. THE CHURCH,
THOSE CHRIST-FOLLOWERS WITH
SPINE AND HEART, REFUSED TO
BE SILENCED, REFUSED TO BE
DRIVEN UNDERGROUND, REFUSED
TO STOP CARRYING THE FIRE.
AT GREAT RISK AND SACRIFICE
THE CHURCH SPOKE TRUTH INTO
THEIR GENERATIONS AND WERE
GOD'S LOVE TO THE WORLD."

How fearless do we dare be? Completely. The testimony of millions of believers through the centuries speaks to the power of the gospel story to our time.

May we be resilient.

May we be fearless.

And may we carry the fire to the next generations.

ESSENTIAL QUESTIONS:

What is your story? Who "carried fire" to you?

Beyond volunteering, what commitments could we make to the next generations?

What power does the gospel story carry in our time?

What cultural fear do you have that you need to believe will "not prevail against it" (God's plan).

THE PRESENCE OF A LOVING, CARING ADULT

CHAPTER 6

If you could give just one gift to every child in the world, what would you choose?

Clean water? Medical care? Food for kids living in poverty? Access to the gospel? Shelter or education? An eradication of poverty?

What choice would you make to have the greatest impact on a child's resilience and future?

Be careful. The answer is not as obvious as it seems. One factor is significantly more impacting than any of the others. In fact, in many cases it creates receptivity to the gospel. The most significant factor in a child's resilience is a strong relationship with a caring adult. Even in the presence of a significant number of risk factors—poverty, hunger challenges, disease, lack of education or even family ties—having a close relationship with a loving, caring adult can help develop the strength a child needs to face significant threats and overwhelming challenges.

My husband, Steve, grew up in a radically loving church. He actually called five women "Mom" in his childhood— his own mother, his pastor's wife, his best friend's mom and two of his aunts—all church women who loved him. Their affection seriously buffered him from some of life's realities. In fact, he was so naïve that it took until his college years before he realized that someone didn't like him! He was shocked!

The presence of caring adults in his life helped him thrive. It is the foundation for a lifetime of resilience. That's why kids will often seek a soul-parent, a parent surrogate, someone who is open to them and will bring them to an emotional and spiritual home.

WHAT CHOICE WOULD YOU MAKE TO HAVE THE GREATEST IMPACT ON A CHILD'S RESILIENCE AND FUTURE?

In March 2015, Harvard's Center on the Developing Child released a study that stated, *"Every child who winds up doing well has had at least one stable and committed relationship with a supportive adult."* [1]

"EVERY CHILD WHO WINDS UP DOING WELL HAS HAD AT LEAST ONE STABLE AND COMMITTED RELATIONSHIP WITH A SUPPORTIVE ADULT."

Children who end up "doing well" are children who had resilience built into their fiber by a loving, caring adult.

The Harvard Study on resilience found that there was also a common set of characteristics that predispose children to positive outcomes in the face of adversity:

The availability of at least one stable, caring, and supportive relationship between a child and an adult caregiver.

A sense of mastery over life circumstances.

Strong executive function and self-regulation skills.

The supportive context of affirming faith or cultural traditions. [2]

Think about it. The church offers all four of these resilience builders to kids facing challenges. Times have so radically changed that the church can no longer assume that parents are these "loving caring" adults in children's lives. We need to ask the hard question, "What about the 100+ million kids in America who have no loving, caring adult at home? Where will they find acceptance, guidance and affirmation?

Be sure of this: Children without spiritual mothers and fathers are orphans. God clearly states His heart towards them, and His desire for the church to be spiritual fathers and mothers to such kids.

We can get this right! And in many places we are already the loving, caring adults in kids' lives. Think about the distinctives the church is already bringing to this issue:

Was someone there for you? Was there a certain person who sweetened your days as a child? Someone whose name you may have forgotten, but who made you feel noticed and special? Someone other than your parents?

Did the Bible teach you mastery over life circumstances through its wisdom? Did you learn from examples like Esther, Daniel, David and Goliath? Did their lives inform your pathway?

Were you taught to master impulses that were potentially self-destructive and sinful, and surrender your life to a better more self-regulated, Spirit-informed way?

Did your faith community affirm and support your decision to live a more resilient life?

The formula for resilience is in the church's DNA! Take a troubled kid, add a loving, caring adult and a gospel-based supportive biblical community and the Nicolas Cruzes of the world will then be guided into another life path other than becoming the triggerman in school shootings.

I know how important a loving, caring adult can be to a child. I had one in my life. I'm not exactly sure how old I was when I began to be interested in her. Honestly, she was so old, I thought she must be a "witch" like I had seen in children's books. She lived next door. I think I must have been 3-years-old. This old woman was unlike anything I had seen before. Using a cane, she maneuvered her bent, darkly clothed body through her adjoining backyard. I knew about witches. I had heard about Hansel and Gretel. So I kept an eye on her just in case she tried anything tricky. But I didn't feel threatened. No, I was interested and attracted. If she ever saw me, she never even said "Hi!" to me.

Repulsion was eventually overcome by my childhood curiosity. One day I found myself climbing the stairs of her gingerbreaded front porch. With pre-school reading ability, I slowly sounded out the sign on her front door. KNOCK ONCE AND COME IN. This is too easy. It must be a trap to get me! But curiosity won out again, I knocked once and walked in—one step.

She came to greet me through a faded mauve and cream wallpapered living room. An eternity seemed to pass as this aged specter labored her way toward me. I've tried to remember her face, but I can't. But I do remember her hands. I was at eye level with blue rivers that popped through an intriguing landscape of wrinkled, transparent skin. I was awestruck. What had happened to her?

In time, I became a regular visitor to the old "witch's" home. She wooed me with shredded wheat, popcorn balls and homemade gingerbread. Everybody called her Grandma Wheaton and so did I. I don't know if she thought I was a pest, but I never remember being asked to leave; she simply integrated me into her life. When she became tired, we each took our naps, playing a game called "Let's see who can go to sleep the quickest." When naps were over, I remember claiming the victory. "I won! I won!" She never won.

And so our unusual friendship began: a child starting life and a woman ending hers. She was a storyteller, and I was her eager audience. She filled our days with stories from her life. She talked about how her young mother had been killed when a train's cowcatcher snagged the hoops of her skirt, pulling her under its grinding wheels and throwing her infant brother up to the smokestack and to his death. Grandma Wheaton had been motherless throughout her childhood.

TOP PHOTO: *Valerie as a child*
BOTTOM PHOTO: *Grandma Wheaton*

There was also a special picture on her mantle. A child wearing a sailor suit looked at us with serious eyes. It was her only child, a boy who died in a flu epidemic. Her life had known an abundance of grief and loss.

Knowing that, I would like to think I wasn't just a pest to her. Maybe God used me to fill some of the lonely gaps in her life. To me, she was much more than a neighbor. She told me about Jesus and His love for children. She softened my heart to come to Him as a 3-year-old. Relationship preceded the gospel and made a way for me to respond to God's love. When she made a space for me to belong in her life, believing followed quickly after. How sweet for me that she was willing to be found "with child" in her advanced age. Looking back, I was probably a daily inconvenience, but maybe I was more. Maybe I was an answer to her Hannah-like prayers for a child. I wish I knew.

Though I do not know if I was more to Grandma Wheaton or not, I can tell you this for certain: through the years her impact has remained with me. She has stuck with me! Sometimes people tell me I'm a good storyteller. I think I probably learned it from her. She is also the reason why I take children's spirituality so seriously.

Here's the thing: even though my parents were believers and loved me deeply, I needed more. I can't even tell you why anymore. I just needed this loving, caring adult woman in my life.

The presence of a loving, caring adult in a child's development is being raised as one of the most pressing needs for today's children across the globe. Both the faith sector and secular experts agree on the importance of this missing factor in many kids' lives.

THE PRESENCE OF A LOVING, CARING ADULT IN A CHILD'S DEVELOPMENT IS BEING RAISED AS ONE OF THE MOST PRESSING NEEDS FOR TODAY'S CHILD ACROSS THE GLOBE.

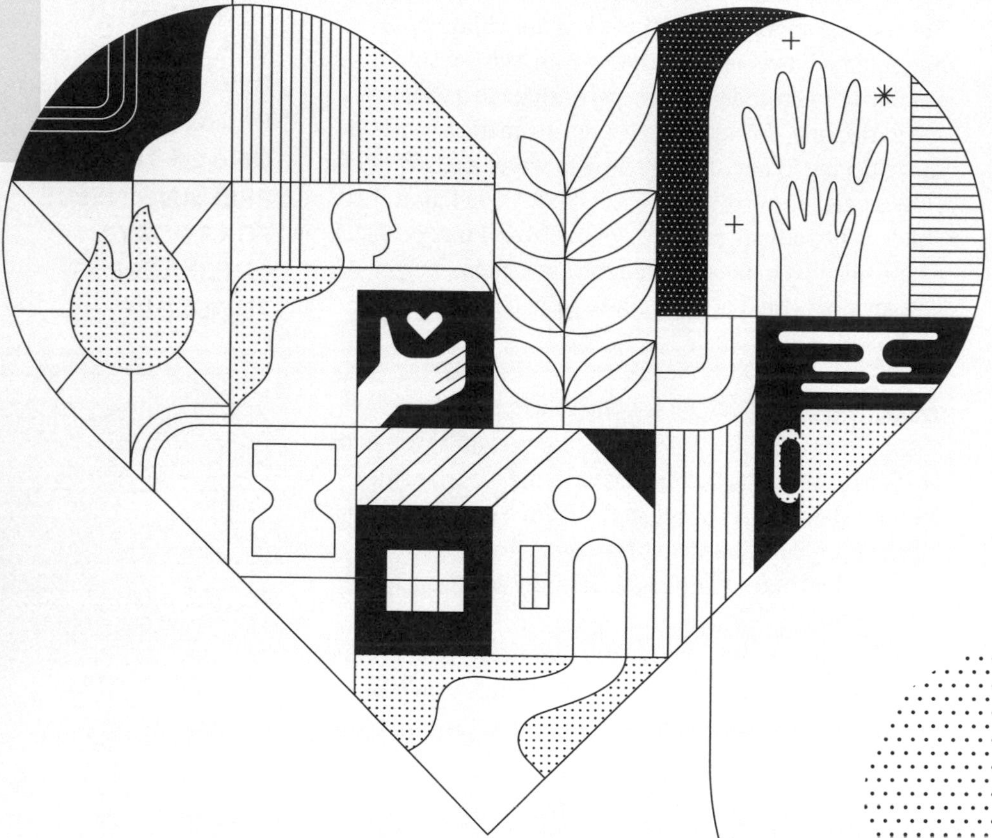

"

THE #1 OUTCOME IN PREDICTING
WHETHER A CHILD IS GOING TO
DO WELL OR NOT ... IT'S NOT
EDUCATION, IT' NOT MONEY,
IT'S NOT HOME. IT'S WHETHER
OR NOT THEY HAVE AN ADULT TO
PUT THEIR ARM AROUND THEIR
SHOULDERS AND SAY, "I'LL WALK
THIS WALK WITH YOU." [3]

Peter Fonagy, the Chief Executive of the Anna Freud National Centre for Children and Families—a mental health charity—has spent more than half a century studying child development. He says:

"My impression is that young people have less face-to-face contact with older people than they once used to. The socializing agent for a young person is another young person, and that's not what the brain is designed for.

"It is designed for a young person to be socialized and supported in their development by an older person. Families have fewer meals together as people spend more time with friends on the internet. **The digital is not so much the problem—it's what the digital pushes out.**" [4]

All sectors of our country agree. We need to reverse the trends of absenteeism in kids' lives! When we minister to children we don't always know how our time will impact the outcome of their lives. Are we making a difference at all? Do we matter? Can one person influence the trajectory of a kid's whole life? The answer to those questions is a resounding yes!

In a recent study by Barna on youth who were classified as resilient disciples from the ages of eighteen to twenty-nine, 77% reported that "When growing up, I had close personal friends who were adults from my church, parish or faith community." [5]

"We are loved into loving Jesus." [5]

Allow me to introduce you to Larry Acosta. Acosta knows how important healthy adult relationships are for kids. Through the Urban Youth Ministries Institute, Larry has led thousands of young men and women in predominately Latino and urban communities to become resilient Jesus followers. However, Larry's life wasn't always as it is today.

Larry grew up in a broken Latino family in a tough urban community in Southern California. Larry's father was a migrant farmworker as a child. His father's childhood was filled with abuse from his own dad. Sadly, those years of mistreatment spilled over into Larry's childhood. As a result, Larry's relationship with his father was also broken and filled with anger and loss.

Yet, in the midst of this chaos and fear, a little church in the area became a place of love, hope and healing. In an unlikely possibility, two older white women began coming into his neighborhood every week to pick him up for church. Every week they intervened in "a little brown boy's life:" (Larry's words). At a time when many of Larry's peers were being introduced to gangs, drugs and dropping out of school, Larry was introduced to Jesus. It was at this church that Larry experienced healthy relationships with men who loved God. For a young man from a home steeped in rage, experiencing the love and care of Christian men made a huge difference in Larry's life. A pair of older white women and a church full of men who cared for him changed the trajectory of Larry's future.

Today Larry credits that church as being the place and space where he was able to encounter the love of Jesus. He belonged. It was through the care of the men and women of this little church that Larry became more than the sum of his circumstances.

But how does this happen? Was there a plan and program in place that made this difference? Yes, the church had an Awana program, but it was more than the Awana ministry and Sunday school that mattered. What made the discipleship difference was people. People who committed to love Larry, to look after him, despite the return and the inconvenience. This is the beauty and power of the local church when it practices discipleship.

There are so many children like Larry in the world, children who find themselves in such difficult situations. But God can provide in miraculous ways for them. I sat in the back of the church during large group time with Awana Clubs Cubbies. They were singing, "My God is so big, so strong and so mighty there's nothing my God cannot do." As they sang, I thought about a little boy from Papua, New Guinea, who needed a mighty and strong God.

He was born to a young woman who was mentally disabled. Due to her disability, she was cast out from her family and slept wherever she could find rest—caves, old unused houses, the streets. But one night someone attacked her and she became pregnant, eventually giving birth to a baby boy, Pamu. No one knows who his father is.

When Pamu was seven months old, he was taken from his mother and given to his grandmother for care. He stayed with her for four years. But he left his grandmother when a cousin told them he would take Pamu and put him in school if he stayed with him. For three years he lived with his cousin. But instead of putting him in school, he used Pamu as child labor in his home. Little Pamu did all the household duties.

When Pamu failed to work hard enough, his cousin sent him back to live with his grandmother. He was still just a little boy, unwanted by everyone. But soon his life would change for the better. A neighbor brought him to Awana club. He became a faithful attender and Christ-follower. But an Awana worker cared for him deeply and soon took him to live with him where he is being sent to school and living happily.

There are many things children like Pamu need, but a loving, caring adult can make the most difference in a child's life.

Think a moment. Is there a child in your life who is picking you? Someone who hangs at your home uninvited? A child at church who comes alone without family? A kid who acts out or who is a loner? Why has God brought that kid into your life or to your attention?

Got a name? Good.

Now ask God, "What would you have me say to this child? What would you have me be to this child? Is there a special role for me to play in this child's life?"

"But," you protest. "I don't even like this kid!"

Right. And understand, that kid might not be that crazy about you either. But feelings follow action. Walk this child's walk for a while. Start to understand this child's life. In time, you are apt to become the loving, caring adult who can potentially make a lifetime of difference for that child just by walking that walk together.

Youprobably won't end poverty. Nor will I. We can't eradicate every disease or end hunger. We can't keep families from dissolving, but there is something we can do that mitigates whatever problem a child is facing. We can be there. We can be the steady presence of the loving, caring adult. Through us children can see what matters the most—the care and love of God and His Son—who gave His life for our sins.

ESSENTIAL QUESTIONS:

Do you know the story of a troubled child whose life was intervened by the presence of a loving, caring adult? Share the story if it's appropriate.

Did you have someone in your life at a time when you were young and needed help?

Put the pieces together. Is a child presenting him or herself to your life in hopes that you will "be there"?

How can adults be the loving, caring presence in kids' lives?

CHURCH BABIES

CHAPTER 7

I was in my happy place, absorbed in the joy of picking ripe ready-to-eat tomatoes and recently-picked golden peaches at a Georgia roadside vegetable stand, when I heard a child's voice saying, "Lady, I really like your blouse. It's very beautiful."

What's this? I thought. In this age of "stranger danger," it's rare for a child to initiate conversation with an adult. I looked up and across the corn bin and saw a little girl, about 9-years-old, smiling at me. She was "decked out" from head to toe. Large pink glasses framed her face. Pigtails shot like fountains over her head and dangled shiny, colorful ornaments from their bases. A large, intricate white and gold choker, bangle bracelets and ornamented tennis shoes completed her ensemble. She was a rainbow of color and life.

We are two peas in a pod—both overdressed—for Sunday afternoon roadside shopping, I thought. This was a T-shirt crowd, but I was dressed in heels and lace stopping on my way home from church.

"Oh," I smiled, "Thank you for saying something.
And I really like your necklace."

"Thank you!" she responded. "I sooo wanted a bigger one, but my mother said it's not appropriate for me."

I was feeling slightly enchanted by now. "Well," I said, "you look fabulous anyway. It all works!"

Later in the car driving home, I thought about that charming little girl. I wished I could have had a little chat with her mom. "Mom," I would have said, "your daughter is an artist, I believe. Do you know, she complimented me on my blouse? Most kids would have missed that, but she sees what others don't. And she is expressive in the only way she can be right now ... her clothes. Someday we'll be buying her art or asking her to help us design our homes. She's got the seeing/expressive gift. How wonderful!"

Budding artists are not the only children who can be missed or misunderstood by parents who are "appropriate." Leaders-in-the-making can be thought of as "bossy" by parents who find themselves embarrassed by their child's "socially-forward" behavior. Introverted children, who may seem overly shy and backward to socially-engaged parents, may be storing things up to become thought leaders one day.

Sometimes it takes a third party to help a parent actually "see" his or her child. I know, because I was "that" parent who needed another set of knowing adult eyes to help me see my child.

When Brendan, our firstborn son, was in third grade, I had walked confidently into his parent-teacher conference. He was smart, adorable and charming. What could go wrong?

"There is something I have to tell you about Brendan," his teacher said. "Every day when the other kids are lined up for lunch Brendan looks up from a project of his own that he is doing at his desk and asks, "Where are we going?"

"Oh no!" the former teacher in me said. "I am so sorry. That must really bother you." I knew it would have bothered me if I were the teacher experiencing that at lunch every day.

"Mrs. Bell, I am not telling you this because Brendan is a problem. I want you to understand something about him. He is not plugged in at school, like most kids are by now, because he has an incredibly rich interior world. School is boring in comparison. His test scores indicate he is gifted, but he is still not reading. We are going to get him special help."

In the 30 years since, I have often thought of that teacher with gratefulness for her huge-get-it factor for my son. Because of her insight, I was shown that he was special, not a problem. Today he is an adult with four young sons of his own. His rich interior world and giftedness is expressing itself these days as a psychotherapist who leads two different counseling practices with more than 30 counselors. Every day he and his team help a lot of "special kids" whose parents need their help to see them accurately.

Some of the most gifted kids can be the ones parents have the hardest time "seeing." In a sense, they are absorbed at their desks with their interior worlds while the rest of the kids their age are lined up for lunch. A story in Scripture confirms this.

In I Samuel 16, Samuel, the prophet of God, has been told to go to Bethlehem, to Jesse's house. God has chosen a new king of Israel to replace Saul from among Jesse's eight sons. One by one (most likely in order of probability in Jesse's mind) Jesse brings seven of his sons to Samuel. But they all are rejected as not being God's choice.

Confused, Samuel asks Jesse, "Are these all the sons you have?"

"There is still the youngest, but he is tending the sheep." Jesse has already measured David and found him wanting. "No way!" We can read Jesse's mind across the centuries to us today.

But look at how David is described when he is brought to Samuel. He is "glowing with health and had a fine appearance and handsome features." Another time a very young David is described as *knowing how to play the lyre. He is a brave man and a warrior. He speaks well and is a fine looking man.*

David had everything he needed to capture, not only the heart of the nation of Israel, but also the heart of God. But his father, Jesse "missed" him.

God explains his choice of David to Samuel. "The Lord does not look at the things people look at. People look at the outward appearance, but the Lord looks at the heart."

KIDS NEED MORE THAN PARENTS … THEY NEED TO BE A PART OF THE LIVING ORGANISM OF FAITH, THE CHURCH.

This is why, though parents are important, even primary, in the spiritual direction and discipleship of their children, they are not "only" or even enough. Children may grow in the soil of their parents' faith, but they need light and air and more.

They need to be "seen" through adult sets of eyes that are less enmeshed than their own parents' eyes. Children need to be known in ways that may escape their parents.

This is just one of the reasons children need the church.

CHILDREN MAY GROW IN THE SOIL OF THEIR PARENTS' FAITH, BUT THEY NEED LIGHT AND AIR AND MORE.

Children Need to be Part of the "Seeing" Faith-Building Church.

Children have so many needs a church can meet. Children need their childhoods celebrated. Follow the laughter at any time in the church and it will lead straight to the children's wing. From where do balloons launch? Where do the skits and songs with actions show up? Where do the most fun adults in a church end up serving? Where the kids are! No one does celebration of kids better than the church!

But so much more than joy is happening for children at church. They are being exposed to the outrageous faith of believers within the body. Children who watch adult believers celebrate eternity while weeping at the edge of a newly dug grave are learning about the hope of eternity. When they lift their young voices and join others in praise of a God none of them has ever seen, but who is real just the same, they are learning the holy enchantment of praise and worship. The week-after-week testimonies of radically changed lives, or accounts of God's miraculous intervention, or stories of supernatural help in a time of need are forming them to trust in God. Maybe they'll witness the tears of a grown man down on his knees at the altar, struggling to submit to God some stubborn area of sin and begin to understand the power of God's forgiveness. When they see people being baptized in their street clothes and filled with God's spirit as they come up out of the waters hugging the pastor with their dripping wet joy, they are learning the beauty of surrender to God. They may watch a "Church Baby"—a baby with special needs who is loved on by the entire congregation—and know they belong and are accepted "as is." When the church exposes them to the needs of the world—the suffering, the hunger, the disease—they may respond and give from their piggy banks, or some young entrepreneurial effort. At church, they join other kids their age who are loving God and bravely making their own counter-cultural journeys. The worshiping face of someone lost in God may draw them to spirituality, even as children. It is within the body of Christ that they are known, spiritually nurtured and made disciples.

All this happens in their lives because there is a church. It doesn't happen at home. It doesn't happen on the screen.

What is more life-giving than experiencing a contagious faith in community ... the feel of it, the lows and highs of it, the supernatural joining togetherness of it? It is not enough to simply give mental assent to a creed, to nod a passive head in agreement, or understand Scripture intellectually. Our souls need to be captured by supernatural love and power. We need to fall in awe and love with Jesus together. We need to help each other and our children know God. The church is the faith engine driving us to God and to each other. The church has been traveling this spiritual journey for thousands of years and is uniquely able to expose children to that corporate faith.

If you were fortunate enough to grow up in the church, what keeps drawing you to it today? I think about that sometimes ... why am I still there? Strangely, I don't remember one sermon from my childhood years in church. What I do cherish is my parents and their friends singing from their church pews as one lifted voice, the reverence my parents and others held for their underlined Bibles, their fervent prayers for each other with "Amen!" and "Yes, Lord!" staccatos. A snapshot in my mind from my childhood is of our pastor asleep on our sofa after a family Sunday meal. Or the wonder I experienced when my father's hands, holding a conductor's baton, fell and the majestic *Hallelujah* chorus of choir and orchestra would fill our church down to our very bones and marrow.

We can't let this generation and those to come of children miss that. Soon, in their adult years, they will need to remember their childhood churches and draw supernatural strength from those memories in order to be spiritually resilient in the world they will inherit.

No matter how spiritually adequate the parents, they can't expose their children to communal faith without the church. Yes, children need their parents spiritually. Parents are primary in a child's faith development. But kids need more than parents. They need more than Bible truths learned on a screen or read in a book. They need to be part of the living organism of faith, the church.

"Well," the lovely Christian woman answered when I asked where she and her family attend church. "Well, we don't. We have our own family church at our home on Sundays. It's really lovely."

I wanted to say, "Oh, I'm so sorry, but what that really is ... is not enough. You may be adequate, but you are still not enough. You are actually depriving your kids. They need the faith of the entire body of Christ to fuel their future strength. You are not enough now and you won't be enough to prepare them to face fearlessly outward in 2050 with a faith that will be unshakeable and unmovable."

In the book, *Sticky Faith* a case is made for the primary position of parents in children's faith walk. Parents are influencers, modelers, and conveyers of faith. But even with this emphasis on the role of parents, *Sticky Faith* encourages parents to develop a "sticky web" of five adults, besides parents, who would walk their child through their faith journey. [1]

What if a church decided to be this kind of faith family for the children who walk through its doors? What if, instead of doing KidMin like the compulsories—running programs, filling the time, entertaining kids spiritually—we developed a new focus, with a greater sensitivity to the 50% of American children who live in single-parent homes? What if church became the second home for all kids? What if we fell in love with kids like we never have before?

I believe everything would change. From the children's wing of the church, a spiritual fire of loving care would spread into the congregation. The church would be revitalized, it would rekindle its desire to reach its community and that would be revival. And it would start with children!

With the shifting landscapes of family decline and heightened cultural influence through technology, how does a church meet children's needs today? How does a church become a "seeing" church—one that helps parents not miss the amazing children right in their own homes.

I BELIEVE EVERYTHING WOULD CHANGE. FROM THE CHILDREN'S WING OF THE CHURCII A SPIRITUAL FIRE OF LOVING CARE WOULD SPREAD INTO THE CONGREGATION.

A "Seeing" Church Understands That This Generation of Children Needs the Church to be Family Like No Modern Generation before Them.

At a time when so many families are struggling, the church has an opportunity to step up its commitment to kids and come alongside the family, but something else seems to be happening. Awana recently initiated an independent study that informed us on the direction church dedication to kids is going. When questioned in this independent poll KidMin leaders answered that the most important factor informing their choice of curriculum was the gospel. Good start!

But the second most important factor informing their choice of curriculum was "Easiness." In fact, all the questions that followed were filled in with things about themselves. It was as if children had disappeared from their awareness and their needs were no longer factoring in. Or if they factored in, it was behind the adult KidMin leader's needs.

Think of this: These responses, showing such a dim passion for children, are from people who are involved in children's ministry! You might expect this less-than-aware response from areas of the church more removed from children, but not from those who are actually working with children and youth. It's critical that the church falls in love with children and the work of God in their lives again. It's time!

A "Seeing" Church Knows More Than a Child's Name. It Knows His or Her Story.

Knowing a child's name is a good start, but it is not the same as really knowing a child.

My grandsons started Awana in the middle of the school year. Rowan, 8 at the time, was assigned to a team whose de facto leader was a bossy little girl. Her vest was covered in badges and jewels. She was a high achiever, a born leader, and she didn't hesitate to boss Rowan around. But even more strangely, he did whatever she said. Maybe it was a crush that caused him to be so cooperative, but whatever, little miss pigtailed bossy boss was in charge.

I thought she was adorable, but it wasn't until large group time that I fell in love with her. The leader asked, "Do you know anyone we should pray for? Her hand shot up. "Please pray for my daddy. He doesn't know Jesus."

There could be a world of pain behind that statement, "He doesn't know Jesus." Rejection. Abandonment. Abuse. So that's when I fell in love with her. Later I would discover the kind of pain hidden in her words about her dad. Thinking back on that night, I wish I had picked up on her cues. I wish I had followed through with her mother to learn this little girl's complete story. It might have made a difference in what happened the next week.

That week was the Awana Grand Prix race car week. And what a serious competition it was! Blocks of wood were shaven and weighted, painted and wheels greased for their ultimate winning speed. Dads, whose reputations were at great stake, stood along the raceway cheering and yelling. Computer generated speeds were posted over the finish line on large screens.

But where was my favorite little pigtailed girl? Missing. She was not there that night. And then it hit me; how could she participate when her father was missing in action? Why weren't we more sensitive to her needs? Where were the father substitutes? Why didn't we try to anticipate her loss? Why wasn't I "tuned in"?

A "Seeing" Church Fills in the Gaps

One of my friends is an excellent carpenter. I also admire his dedication to his family. "Kevin, you're such a great dad!" I find myself telling him from time to time. Recently, his Facebook post captured his three little girls helping him lay tile. It made me smile, but knowing his story, I have a deeper appreciation for what this means in his life. His father abandoned Kevin and his mother when he was very young. But there was a church ... a "seeing" church! Both Kevin and his mom were loved on by a young childless couple. When there were projects around the house, this young husband included Kevin. The gap of fatherlessness in Kevin's life was filled by this "knowing" young Christian couple. That's where he learned how to be a great dad.

Knowing a child's circumstances can soften our responses to their behavior. An Awana missionary told me that she was very challenged by the behavior of a young boy at club. During game time, he was "hands on" all the other kids, starting fights, picking on smaller kids. This behavior kept up throughout the night ... every week. Finally, in exasperation she asked him, "Hey, Kirk, why are you such a handful"?

Without a pause, Kirk said, "It's because I'm hungry."

She hadn't "seen" that gap. She didn't "know" his story.

"

I BELIEVE EVERYTHING WOULD CHANGE. FROM THE CHILDREN'S WING OF THE CHURCH A SPIRITUAL FIRE OF LOVING CARE WOULD SPREAD INTO THE CONGREGATION. THE CHURCH WOULD BE REVITALIZED, IT WOULD REKINDLE ITS DESIRE TO REACH ITS COMMUNITY AND THAT WOULD BE REVIVAL. AND IT WOULD START WITH CHILDREN!"

The next week she provided pizza for Kirk and his brother and sister. The problem was resolved. The "hyper" activity stopped.

It made her think, "Could the rest of these kids be hungry too?"

The next week it was Awana and pizza for everyone! Now these kids can look forward to being fed and being a part of a "seeing" church every week.

Sometimes an entire "seeing" church fills the gaps. Friends of ours were parents of a severely handicapped baby. Her life expectancy was only a few months. It was a heartbreaking and exhausting time in their lives. But they didn't carry the burden alone. Every week their church came alongside them, "adopting" their baby and helping them carry their heartbreak. Every Sunday, week after week, she was passed from loving arms to loving arms. The church walked her to sleep in the nursery. They sang to her and prayed over her. They carried her until her parents were able to hunt her down after church. Every Sunday she was everyone's baby. Our friends smiled that they never knew who might be caring for her at any particular time. This church meant so much to our friends. They called their baby the "Church Baby."

Because there was a church, the heartbreak was bearable.

Every child deserves to be the Church Baby ... to be "seen" and loved despite his or her behavior or life circumstances, to be known and celebrated by a church family. Whatever the situation, the church can sweeten a child's life.

A "Seeing" Church Commits to Praying Regularly for Every Child in the Church, Neighborhood and Surrounding Communities.

Take your list of kids to God by name. Who is acting out? Who is struggling in school? Are there signs that they might be hungry? Who is fatherless? What parents are facing unemployment or medical bills and might be struggling to make ends meet?

Then spread out your prayers. Is there a neighborhood surrounding your church? Pray that those kids would come through the church doors and that they would be the first of their families to come to Christ. Is there a problem in your community affecting children—drugs, poverty, unemployment, fatherlessness, ineffective public schools? Lift the children affected by those kinds of things to God and pray your church will be able to minister to them.

Prayer changes everything. Prayers start renewal of God's people. Praying softens our hearts.

Lastly, a "Seeing" Church Helps Parents Grasp Their Children's Spiritual Potential.

I develop crushes on churches. I know it's funny, but sometimes a church just becomes Jesus in their communities and I am drawn to them.

Salem Baptist Church in Dalton, Georgia, is one of those churches. It has a unique mission statement. It is only one word, "Others." It's a great vision, but as most of us have experienced, it is one thing to have a vision and another completely to live it out. This church lives it out. Here's how: Recently, their Awana club leaders decided that no child would come to club and leave without hearing the gospel. This focus resulted in an end-of-the-year baptismal service that was just for the 43 kids who had come to Christ that year ... all because of their leadership's decision to focus on the gospel.

Now the caring, loving adult KidMin leaders of Salem Baptist Church were jazzed. They wanted to do more, but club was finished for the year and would not start up again until the fall.

"What about the kids in the nearby trailer park? They don't come to church. They don't know the gospel!" That's when they started "Awana in the Streets." Every week, their children would run up to the trailer doors, knock and invite the resident children to come play games and have hot dogs or pizza and hear the story of God's love.

At the beginning of the following fall I asked, "How many kids ended up coming to club at your church because of "Awana in the Streets?"

They said, "Eight kids!" I thought, Only *eight kids?* But they weren't disappointed. They were thrilled! That was eight new families they were able to reach. Eight kids who were lost without the church and Christ.

KIDMIN LEADERS ARE PERFECTLY PLACED TO HELP PARENTS SEE THEIR CHILDREN'S POTENTIAL IN WAYS THEY HAVE NOT PREVIOUSLY SEEN THEM.

They weren't done yet though. They were ready for more. "What about the kids far away, in some other country? They don't know the gospel!" That's when they became involved in "Verse-a-thon." It's like a marathon, but it's all done by memory verses...sponsored memory verses. Each child found sponsors for the number of memory verses they could recite in one sitting. And here's the thing: Grandma and Grandpa had no idea how many verses their "darlings" could recite! It's a beautiful fundraising dream! When the night was over and hundred of verses were recited, Salem Baptist Church kids had raised more than $7,000 to equip and train leaders in Honduras to reach kids. That reaches 700 kids and trains over 20 churches in how to reach and disciple children! The kids at Salem Baptist Church practically "own" Honduras!

Who knew kids could be so evangelistic, entrepreneurial and driven to reach out? Children are nearly always more than we realize they can be. KidMin leaders are perfectly placed to help parents to see their children's potential in ways they have not previously seen them.

Now when Salem Baptist Church looks at their children, they see disciples, evangelists, missionaries and kingdom entrepreneurs. They see kids who, even at their young ages, can make an impact for an entire country like Honduras.

But what if kids could actually turn a country around? The most striking example of kids living out an awesome spiritual potential is happening right now in a country I can't name for security reasons. This country has been war torn for decades. During those years, the Christian witness and church has been minimized, persecuted and driven underground. But a stateside church could not forget that country. They cared and gave Awana $60,000 to translate materials into the country's language. In the ten years since that gift was given, there are now 60,000 kids coming to those Awana clubs. Most of these kids are becoming first generation believers! I was told they often fall to their knees when they accept God's love and Jesus as their Savior ... it's just too wonderful for their bodies to endure!

I was so touched when I heard this God story that I insisted on visiting and seeing what God was doing. I attended their clubs and the most striking thing was ... I never heard an adult voice "in charge." All the leadership, from the stage and with the small groups: was done by children 12-, 13-, 14-, 15-years-old! These amazing children had been trained to lead because there was not an older generation of believers from which to draw.

The global church has barely touched children's potential for the kingdom. Perhaps it's time we started "seeing" children in the full light of who God created them to be:

Missionaries

Evangelists

Entrepreneurs for the kingdom

Leaders

Influencers of a generation

OUT OF THE MOUTHS OF BABES AND SUCKLING HAST THOU ORDAINED STRENGTH.

Psalm 8:2 (KJV)

My grandmother had a favorite hymn. She would sing it as she worked around our house.

> *There's a church in the valley by the wildwood,*
> *No lovelier spot in the dale;*
> *No place is so dear to my childhood,*
> *As the little brown church in the vale.*
>
> *Oh come to the church in the wildwood,*
> *Oh, come to the church in the dale,*
> *No spot is so dear to my childhood,*
> *As the little brown church in the vale.*

Even into her old age, her life was blessed because there was a church in her childhood. Even as a young child I could hear the longing in her voice as she sang. I knew the church was special.

May this generation of children remember the "little brown churches in the vales" of their own childhoods and from those memories find the courage and strength to lead the church and influence the culture in their adult years.

Because there was a church ...

ESSENTIAL QUESTIONS:

If you have a "but there was a church" story, share it at
www.ResilientDisciples.com

*What church memories have traveled into your adult life as
life-giving and foundational to your faith?*

*Why does the church matter today? Why does the church
matter in 2050?*

*Get inspired! Ask other people to share their "but there was
a church" stories.*

The Crucial Question:
IS KIDMIN WORKING?

CHAPTER 8

As we've journeyed the pages of this book together, your bravery has emerged.

Let's face it, the very thought that the ways of Jesus and the community of the church could be pushed to the margins of society in North America can be a paralyzing idea. Yet, little by little we see it happening through the media, in our universities, in entertainment, in the legal systems and perhaps even right in your own home.

As challenging as it is to discuss adults facing hardship and adversity for their faith in Jesus, it seems far more painful to imagine our children suffering negative impact for their faith in Christ. What will this potential future mean for our children? What changes do we need to make to prepare these precious kids for their future? Imagine this: you are at your local children's ministry gathering. The normal topics have come up–leadership, volunteers, and curriculum—but deep inside, we are all wanting to have a different type of conversation. Will anyone bring it up? Will the silence ever be broken?

This is the moment God has granted each of us, and we can't shy away from it. He's given you a brave and courageous faith to break this silence. To enter into the conversation and to keep pushing forward as you think, dream, and pray for the long-term impact of your ministry and the church of 2050.

WHAT CHANGES DO WE NEED TO MAKE TO PREPARE THESE PRECIOUS KIDS FOR THEIR FUTURE?

In Chapters Five, Six, and Seven we've told stories, described artistic beauty and given a depiction of child and youth discipleship. As we carefully crafted these chapters, we envisioned that we were painting a portrait. A masterpiece. And that masterpiece is *you.*

> You are the Fire Carrier.
> You are the Loving, Caring Adult.
> You are the Church.

At a time in our history when kids need face-to-face discipleship, so many churches have moved the opposite direction. Yet you have a powerful story burning within you, and you are carrying the light to kids and families. You, and your team of disciple makers, are the loving, caring adults who are the lifeline to kids who feel invisible and unknown. You. Are. The. Church. And to the many kids who live in the carnage of brokenness of our secular culture, when they see you and your highly relational church community they see something radiant, beautiful, and even irresistible.

So what's unique about this painting? What's different about the type of child discipleship we are describing? Belonging. **The effective disciple making church of the future will distinctly and specifically elevate giving kids a place to "belong" in a world of increasing isolation and the reordering of community.**

I've Found My People

A couple of years ago, my (Matt) youngest son Hudson joined Katie and me at a Board of Directors dinner. It was so interesting to watch him at age 13 to interacting with each of the high capacity adults on our board around the dinner table. He was answering questions, asking questions, cracking jokes. This guy was on the team! On the drive home, breaking the silence in the car, he said, "Dad, don't get me wrong, I love my friends. But I think I found my people. I loved hanging out with that group of adults tonight. They were so filled with life!" Katie and I have referred back to that conversation many times. He found this group of loving, caring adults to be irresistible. He was engaged, challenged and captivated. He found belonging.

Today's kids are starving for real, authentic, relational engagement that leads them to a place where they say, "I've found my people." In the Gospels we see Jesus being highly relational. Asking questions. Telling stories. Eating meals. Sharing the best news ever—the truth and hope of the gospel—that He is the very source of life. He was the One who had come to fulfill the law, to save them from their sin and redeem them as His people. And He let them know Him personally. He was the carrier of everlasting fire, the perfect loving, caring adult, and the church embodied. He invited them to true belonging.

The child-loving church of 2050 will be marked by belonging—defined as "highly relational ministry led by loving, caring adults."

In the past decades, we could rely on belonging to take place in a variety of environments within the community because we relied on living in a majority Christian culture. But in 2050, as the cultural gap widens, we will need to be far more relational as advocates for Christ who engage the community and translate and interpret the message of the gospel in a post-Christian or even anti-Christian culture.

In the pages afollowing, let's think, dream and imagine together. Let's define some terms, evaluate what we do and be captivated by the idea of a child discipleship model where belonging (highly relational discipleship) invites kids to believing in Jesus and becoming more like Him.

TODAY'S KIDS ARE STARVING FOR REAL, AUTHENTIC, RELATIONAL ENGAGEMENT THAT LEADS THEM TO A PLACE WHERE THEY SAY, "I'VE FOUND MY PEOPLE."

Your Unique Context

Before we dive deep into "what's working" and "defining success," let's clarify: every church is unique, and that includes yours. While we can see common objectives that are unifying, the dynamics from church to church can be different. Due to that, you will always be the most informed voice in the evaluation of your ministries, and we are honored to be able to walk alongside of you through the thoughts in this book.

Personally, I've had the privilege of being a member at various churches ranging in size from 125 members to over 5000 members. This is also true for my *RESILIENT* co-authors. We've been given the gift of seminary and Bible college degrees, and we have served on staff at churches. We have been church planters and we are local church consultants. Our collective experience has taught us to think scale and effectiveness.

So we hear you when you unpack the challenges of leading a sizable team of paid staff members who engage a group of volunteers that leads hundreds of kids each week. We understand what it's like to lead a small or mid-sized volunteer team that may engage 100+ kids. You may be on the very front lines, directly leading 12 or 25 kids each week, and we've been there too. So as we navigate this conversation together, these two truths sit side by side: Your unique context matters, as do the common objectives that unify all of us. Your context makes you unique compared to a different church in a different community, but we all share the same objective—make resilient disciples. As a community, let's intentionally learn from each other. Let's share our best ideas and be inspired by what's working.

YOUR UNIQUE CONTEXT MATTERS, AS DO THE COMMON OBJECTIVES THAT UNIFY ALL OF US.

What is KidMin?

As KidMin leaders, you know that we do not have a commonly held or centralized definition of "Kids Ministry" that guides how we implement ministry to children in our various contexts. Certainly we have common assumptions relating to major themes such as discipleship, evangelism, entertainment, worship, games, large groups and small groups, etc. However, the way we implement the vision of our ministries is different and unique from church to church. This can make it challenging when we speak of "KidMin" in such general and broad terms.

In our ongoing pursuit to best understand and serve the KidMin community, we've commissioned four research projects in the last few years (each conducted by an independent research firm). In a study we published in 2014 with over 1,000 respondents, we measured "Importance versus performance of producing children who are committed disciples." What exactly does that mean? Well here's an example. As a KidMin community, our survey respondents rated the "importance of producing children who are committed disciples" as a 4.78 out of 5; however, respondents rated their actual performance as a 3.48. [1] The high importance rating on "producing committed disciples" is encouraging; we truly desire to make disciples of the children that we serve. But our performance is an indication that we aren't hitting the mark. Our self reporting "slightly above average" performance is our collective groan to be more effective.

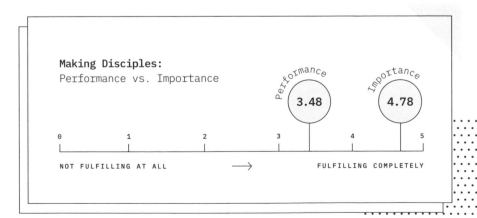

Making Disciples:
Performance vs. Importance

Performance 3.48   Importance 4.78

0   1   2   3   4   5

NOT FULFILLING AT ALL → FULFILLING COMPLETELY

"I FEAR WE MAY REALIZE TOO LATE THAT WE GAVE THEM THINGS THAT DIDN'T REALLY MATTER, THINGS THAT DIDN'T TRAVEL INTO THEIR ADULT LIVES AS ANYTHING MORE THAN SPIRITUAL ENTERTAINMENT AND MORALISTIC STORIES."

In this same study, children's ministry leaders and practitioners vulnerably admitted the fear that they may have sacrificed substance for fun and entertainment. Get this—"Having fun" is the only category where children's ministry leaders outperformed their rating of importance. As a community, we rated "having fun" as a 3.82, but acknowledged that we were actually performing at a 3.95. [2] Let's sit in that for a minute: our behavior is indicating that "having fun" is more important than we actually believe. Don't misunderstand me, we should be having fun—we work with kids! Children's Ministry will forever be the most exciting space in the church. Yet, we wonder if our emphasis on "entertainment" with today's kids programming will result in the long-term fruit we had hoped. This research echoes the concern that Valerie shared in Chapter 2, "I fear we may realize too late that we gave them things that didn't really matter, things that didn't travel into their adult lives as anything more than spiritual entertainment and moralistic stories, things lacking real spiritual power and proactive purpose."

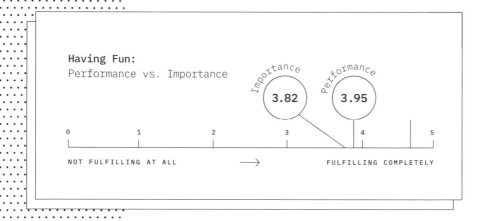

Having Fun:
Performance vs. Importance

Importance 3.82   Performance 3.95

0   1   2   3   4   5

NOT FULFILLING AT ALL   ⟶   FULFILLING COMPLETELY

More recently, in a 2019 unpublished study an independent research firm conducted two different surveys on our behalf with 687 total KidMin respondents. In one of the surveys, we asked the question, "When you are making decisions about curriculum, resources, and materials for children's ministry at your church, what are the most important factors that influence you to choose one over another?" We were encouraged that "Bible/Gospel Based" was rated as the top response with 67% of the respondents placing this as the most important factor. Want to guess what the second highest response was? Perhaps you may think that it was about discipleship? Or kid focused? Helping kids navigate and engage culture? Nope, the second highest response was "Easy to Use/Low Prep." Don't get me wrong; no one wants a "complicated to use" curriculum. But out of all of the places our minds and hearts could go, we made the statement—could you just make it easier for the adults?

These three data points (representative of **many** others we have collected) have been significant to our learning curve because they each reveal something about where we are in children's ministry today.

1
We have a heart to make child disciples, but we see room for significant improvement.

2
We fear that we may have placed too much emphasis on things that don't contribute to long-term child discipleship.

3
We can sometimes make decisions based on what's best for the adults, not what's best for the child's discipleship journey.

So what is KidMin? What is children's ministry? Rather than being a singular idea, KidMin is more of a broad spectrum of many ideas. Kids ministry is being applied by a variety of church leaders who place emphasis on a number of different priorities. Some place high emphasis on Bible teaching, but a lower emphasis on relationships. Other churches place significant emphasis on a highly produced, entertaining and engaging large group time, but less emphasis on robust gospel-based teaching. Other churches value engaging small groups with Bible memory, but less emphasis on kids worship or prayer. There are numerous profiles of what KidMin can look like.

If an experienced consultant evaluated 100 churches with the criteria below, the aforementioned multiple profiles would emerge and we could view ourselves on this spectrum.

How would you rank the importance of the following?

	LOW IMPORTANCE $\longrightarrow$ HIGH IMPORTANCE				
Evangelism	◯	◯	◯	◯	◯
Discipleship	◯	◯	◯	◯	◯
Volunteers	◯	◯	◯	◯	◯
Parent Engagement	◯	◯	◯	◯	◯
Worship	◯	◯	◯	◯	◯
Philosophy	◯	◯	◯	◯	◯
Small Groups	◯	◯	◯	◯	◯
Large Groups	◯	◯	◯	◯	◯
Gospel Focus	◯	◯	◯	◯	◯
Prayer	◯	◯	◯	◯	◯
System	◯	◯	◯	◯	◯
Child Protection	◯	◯	◯	◯	◯
Volunteer Equipping	◯	◯	◯	◯	◯
Missions	◯	◯	◯	◯	◯
Fun & Games	◯	◯	◯	◯	◯
Videos	◯	◯	◯	◯	◯
Scripture Memory	◯	◯	◯	◯	◯
Tracking Success	◯	◯	◯	◯	◯

KidMin is a spectrum of the various ways we minister to and engage children in the local church. It is a broadly used term that encapsulates many approaches to ministry to kids. The positive to this is that it gives us a common term for a broad idea (kids ministry). **But with the mounting cultural divide and a vision to prepare our kids to lead the church of 2050, we are concerned that a broadly defined direction will not help prepare the future leaders of the church.**

What if...

> *What if we fine-tuned our focus?*
>
> *What if we could unite as a community and take the conversation even deeper?*
>
> *What if we could evaluate our long-term success? What would we be willing to let go of to pursue lifelong discipleship for the children we serve?*

In our pursuit to better understand "ministry success" we've been asking a lot of questions, sharing a lot of coffee, and doing a lot of listening. Let's dig into what we are learning.

Defining and Evaluating Success

In one of our two 2019 research projects, we wanted to understand how children's ministry leaders rate "success." When we asked KidMin leaders to "define success in children's ministry," you can see their top three responses to the right.

33.2%
Discipleship

30.6%
Spiritual Growth

28.6%
Salvation

There were no major surprises here, as these results were very similar to what we captured in some studies we conducted in 2013 and 2014.

Then we asked the KidMin respondents to rate the overall success and impact of the children's ministry at their church using a 5 point scale (1 being not successful at all and 5 being very successful). The mean score resulted in a 3.65, which would be considered "fairly successful." When we asked "Why do you view your children's ministry so successfully?" the top result was "Kids are Learning" with 47.6% of the respondents indicating this and the second highest was "Volunteers" at 26.7%. The third highest response was "Parent Involvement" coming in at 15.2% of the respondents indicating.

So let's summarize this concisely: children's ministry leaders who viewed their ministries as being more successful defined success through the lens of highly engaged kids, volunteers and parents.

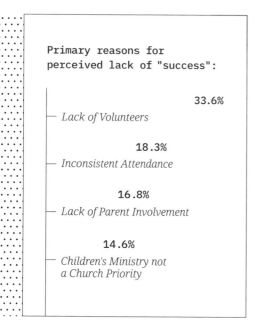

Primary reasons for
perceived lack of "success":

33.6%
— Lack of Volunteers

18.3%
— Inconsistent Attendance

16.8%
— Lack of Parent Involvement

14.6%
— Children's Ministry not
a Church Priority

But there was another group, a segment of the survey who didn't view their children's ministry as being successful. The top four primary reasons can be seen in the chart to the left.

What do you see here with this group of churches? You are probably seeing the same thing we are seeing—a lack of engagement and vitality.

Less successful KidMin ministries are characterized by lower levels of volunteer engagement, lower levels of attendance, lower levels of parental engagement and an underwhelming amount of support from church leadership.

The reality is, if we could follow these churches on their journey, without some level of catalytic or Holy Spirit change, these churches may be closing their doors in the next five or 10 years. This is incredibly sad. What has happened? How have they lost their heart for the gospel and their vision for reaching their own kids?

Not only did we want to understand how a KidMin leader views his ministry as being more or less successful, we also followed up these questions by asking, "How carefully are you and your team evaluating, tracking and measuring the success and impact of the overall children's ministry at your church?" This is where it begins to get even more interesting. The mean score came in right at 2.99 on a 5-point scale.

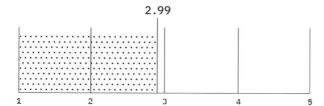

2.99

That score barely hits just below average. For those KidMin leaders who do evaluate, measure and track, they shared that they are using a subjective internal system to analyze (19.7%) paired with church attendance (18.9%).

Many of the respondents vulnerably expressed their frustration. Part of our survey collected information from leaders through open-ended questions. In our open ended and qualitative response mechanisms, we heard the following frustrations related to "evaluating success:"

"We haven't consistently figured out a way to qualitatively measure or track success over the long run."

"We don't have a tool in place to specifically measure our impact just yet."

"We haven't defined specific markers to look for and track as far as impact."

"We lack the knowledge of what and how to track."

"Success is difficult to track. We do keep track of the number of kids involved in each program."

Reality:
The reality is KidMin leaders scored themselves as below average on evaluating, tracking and measuring the overall impact of their kid's ministry.

The primary reasons for the lack of evaluation, tracking and measuring are:

25.8%
Difficult to Evaluate

22.5%
No Tool to Evaluate

16.8%
Lack of Volunteers

So how are we doing? Clearly we know how to run engaging programs and events, but what is the long-term impact of our ministries and how can we evaluate the impact and outcomes?

The answer seems to be, **"We don't quite know."**

EMBRACE THE HUMILITY NEEDED TO ADMIT WHEN WE DON'T KNOW

You may be thinking what we are thinking—"this is super frustrating!" There is so much amazing leadership capacity, energy, brainpower, passion, creativity and grit in KidMin. The children's ministry capacity in North America is such a force for the gospel and yet we "don't quite know" how we are doing. We are not sure what the score is. And we are "average," at best, at evaluating our effectiveness.

Among our team, we've been wrestling with this for some time. One of the greatest leadership lessons we have learned is to embrace the humility needed to admit when we don't know. There is no shame in admitting what we don't know, and then using resources and mentors to help reveal the truth. This is the place where we have found ourselves as a community. This leads to the next powerful question: what are we going to do about the fact that we don't know?

We have a recommendation. Actually, it's more of a rally cry. We need to:

Clarify our target, mission and calling.

We have to narrow the focus of our conversation to "child discipleship." We would even say, Resilient Child Discipleship.

A Clear and Unifying Target,
Mission and Calling–Resilient Child Discipleship

Several years ago, my (Matt) mom who lives in Northern Indiana was on a weekend shopping trip with some of her friends. Their destination? Indianapolis. She said the ladies were having a terrific time talking, telling stories, and laughing it up. When they pulled into the city and saw the St. Louis Arch, they knew there was a problem. Honestly, as a person who is gifted in instinctual navigation, this one is a real head scratcher for me– how did this happen?!?! Not sure. But it is so funny!

I sometimes wonder as we lead in a post Christian and perhaps even anti-Christian culture, where the KidMin community will be in five years or even 10 years. As the cultural gap widens, and further marginalizes the church, in the years ahead, we will need to continue to clarify and refine our target in context to our surroundings.

As we think about this future, we will need to think more specifically than "KidMin." We will need to think more specifically than "we do children's ministry." If the target remains so generally described, than we will continue to "not quite know" how we are doing. It's simply not specific enough. The spectrum is too broad. And when the mission and target are not very specific, we end up at the wrong destination, in a culture that is very different than where we began.

But if we clarify our mission as **Resilient Child Discipleship** then we can create a very specific target. And when you have a specific target, you can build a better plan to hit the target. So below we have two definitions. The first one is a Child Disciple (the "who"). The second one is a definition of Resilient Child Discipleship (the "what" and "how").

Child Disciple

A child who loves Jesus for the rest of his or her life.

Resilient Child Discipleship

The process of a Christ-follower committing meaningful, intentional, and consistent time and space to a child or a group of children so that they may know who Jesus is and are known by a body of believers (**Belong**), to place their faith in Jesus and apply the Word of God (**Believe**), and to reproduce their own discipleship (**Become**) so that a third spiritual generation can lead and love like Jesus Christ.

An extremely important question we need to examine carefully is: What is our "success rate" in producing resilient disciples? David Kinnaman's research in *Faith for Exiles* indicates that the number of resilient disciples remains at only 10%. He describes these resilient disciples as "Christ-followers who (1) attend church at least monthly and engage with their church more than just attending worship services; (2) trust firmly in the authority of the Bible; (3) are committed to Jesus personally and affirm He was crucified and raised from the dead to conquer sin and death; and (4) express desire to transform the broader society as an outcome of their faith." [3]

But what if this number of resilient disciples, instead of 10% was 20%? Or even 30%? What would be the collective impact of that kind of transformation in our culture? To have double or even triple the number of resilient Christ-followers sharing the gospel, living on mission for Christ and bringing His restoration to our broken culture through compassion ministry, justice works and cultural engagement?

This is a captivating calling!

It's a target we can aim for, and a mission we can work toward and pray about together.

An Invitation to Unite

So what would it take for us to unite around a common goal for child discipleship? What if our rally cry as the KidMin community was to elevate the mission and calling of not just children's ministry or KidMin, but of child discipleship?

It's strategic.
It's future focused.
It's intentional.
It's thoughtful.
It's biblical.

On the one hand, I think we all would say, "Well of course we are about 'child discipleship.' That's why we got into ministry in the first place." And this is so true! You got into children's ministry because you see the value. You know the impact that the gospel has in your own life and you believe that children's ministry is the most fruitful, strategic and future-forward ministry of the local church. But a more specific and defined target of "child discipleship" means that we have to ask different questions and we need to reevaluate the pathway. Why? The church of 2050 is going to require a different kind of resilient disciple to lead the church. And a pathway that's not clearly defined and designed around child discipleship will not get us there.

2050

The church of 2050 is going to require a different kind of resilient disciple.

In his book *Essentialism*, Greg McKeown challenges his readers that there are very few key contributing factors that actually lead to organizational success and transformation. It's not the many details (tasks, objectives, etc.) that matter, it's the few. In the book he describes an overcrowded work schedule that is jam packed with a lot of tasks and assignments that don't actually make a significant contribution to the scorecard or the mission of the organization. [4]

WHAT IF THE KIDMIN COMMUNITY DECIDED TO UNITE TOGETHER AS ESSENTIALISTS?

So Greg decided to buck the system. He decided to elevate the few numbers of tasks that contributed toward impact and to diminish (and in some cases stop doing) the tasks that were nonessential to his role and the mission of the organization. Greg found that his impact and the organization's success factors increased.

What if we determined as a community to focus in on the simple factors that contribute to long-term discipleship in the lives of kids? Could we cut through the clutter and abandon the tasks that steal our time yet yield low results? WOW—imagine the collective impact!

In the remaining chapters we are going to discuss an effective child discipleship model built on belonging, believing, and becoming. But before we get there, let's begin to think through how we shift from where we are today, to where we need to be in a more effective future of making resilient disciples. As we think about what it would take to go from where we are today, to a united future elevating child discipleship, KidMin practitioner and child discipleship thought leader, Chris Marchand, is going to walk us through a pathway to implementation.

A PATHWAY TO IMPLEMENTATION

Five Practical Steps

As a green-horned youth pastor, I (Chris) had just finished what I thought was one of my best talks. You know the feeling, right? I was packing everything up to join my teens in "big church" when one of my small group boys came up to me. He said, "You know Pastor Chris—you're really not funny at all. And I don't know if you know this, but your stories are pretty lame, and nobody likes them." Then this young man turned around and walked upstairs to the sanctuary. WOW! I didn't go to church that morning. I sat in the empty fellowship hall and on one hand, I was thankful that someone was brave enough to tell me the truth, but also reeling from the fact that I cannot make disciples with a toolbox filled with anecdotes.

Why did he tell me this? What do you think he was really longing for? I think this young man was asking me to come alongside of him to help him and his comrades develop shared stories together. I mean, making people laugh is great, but what children and youth want today is a better journey. They want their champions to help take them to places they haven't been before. I love a good story and child discipleship is about bringing them into a grander story. They want to meet someone who has broken out of the simulation of church and has seen the effectiveness of God and His people on a global level. They want to know that transformation isn't a myth or something that happened to those special people in Hebrews 11. They want to know that all this information matters. They want to know this lesson is for a purpose.

As KidMin leaders, children's pastors, youth leaders and child influencers, we have our hearts set on discipling kids, but our ministry programming may not be set up to accomplish this vision. So how do we move from where we are, today, to a more effective future that will produce the resilient disciples to lead the church of the future? This is how we break through the silence. We're going to take the next few pages to walk through a pathway to implementation marked with five practical steps. And as you may suspect, it all begins with the "Why."

Start with the "Why"

After more than 15 years in children, youth, and family ministry, I have witnessed thousands of child pick-ups—that moment when a parent brings the security sticker or tag into the room. Like you, I pay attention to those interactions because I always want to make sure a kid goes home with the right adult. But it also gives a brief window into what's going on underneath the surface of a child's life as well as into the minds of the parents. I've seen kids run to the door and wrap their arms around their favorite person in the world. I've seen kids sit with their feet wrapped around stainless steel legs of chairs because they don't want to leave. I've seen parents say, "let's go!" "You're making me late." And I've seen countless parents ask a question that is actually an unstated metric of children's ministry—"Did you have fun!?" After all, we work with kids—we are good at putting on fun programming!

The question "Did you have fun?" is not a terrible question. It's a natural response as we see our kids bound out of their classrooms with a smile on their face (most of the time :). It's just not the most important or the final question. We want kids to enjoy themselves as they engage at church and as they become disciples of Jesus. We want them to form impressions and memories that being with the people of God is a safe harbor in a world filled with violent storms. We want kids to run to church as the place where they are seen, known, and understood better than any other place on the planet.

But why? Why is "did you have fun?" the wrong question to lead with? First, it demonstrates to a child that fun is the most important metric of their time at church. They may begin to ask themselves, Did I have fun? Was I supposed to have fun? Is church always fun? In my almost two decades of vocational church ministry, I've learned what you have probably also learned as well —that church is not always fun. As these children mature, they are going to see that being the church and living out the mission of the church—it is both our greatest joy, but also some of our deepest pain as we walk alongside those who are hurting as we live out the mission of the church. Being a disciple means being connected to pain, struggle and sadness. As pastors, we help celebrate births and hold hands with loved ones beside fresh dug graves. We stand before young couples as they say, "I do." And we also watch families rip themselves apart like ships breaking up underwater. It's not always fun and we need to set the right tone for children, from the earliest of days. We need a better question, because if we don't, we are suggesting that church is some kind of simulation. And this simply won't work for the church of 2050.

So why do we minister to kids? Why do we have a children's ministry? It's because you want to see these kids love Jesus for the rest of their lives. And as we stated earlier, you want to see them believing in, belonging to and becoming like Jesus. Just imagine if our "why" was abundantly clear to church leadership, child disciple makers, parents and kids. Imagine if we were all speaking one language, with unity and clarity. You can just envision a new set of questions and exclamations:

> *Oh, Emma, I missed you! Did you learn about the love of Jesus today?*

> *Hey Garret! Did you experience Jesus today?*

> *I just love watching you become more like Jesus!*

> *I heard you were worshipping God in here today—you inspire me!*

> *Your leader said you helped a friend today.*
> *It's so encouraging to watch you live like Jesus.*

Let's keep being laser focused on our "why" and equip leadership, parents and kids to join in on our common rally cry—Resilient Child Discipleship.

Develop a Kid-Focused Philosophy

As a part of my ministry role, I travel frequently; speaking, leading workshops and consulting with churches. Inevitably, as often as I travel, I run into occasional negative customer service experiences with the airlines. During these encounters I sometimes find myself wondering, "Are your policies and practices designed around what's best for the airline? Or for what's best for getting passengers to their destinations?" In a similar way, I think KidMin leaders feel this tension as well, sometimes wondering if our ministry is designed to help kids arrive at the intended destination— lifelong disciples of Jesus, or something else entirely.

One critical question we've been asking is:
Are we programming the immediate, or prioritizing the future?

SOMETIMES OUR PROGRAMMING CAN OVERTAKE OUR VISION & THE PRIORITY OF FUTURE DISCIPLESHIP

As children's ministry leaders, we can focus the bulk of our energy on the programs that keep kids moving, filled with energy and excitement, but kids can still walk out of our care and be left feeling unknown, isolated, disconnected from the church and having no space to hear from God. Sometimes our programming can overtake our vision and the priority of future discipleship. We have all been there. It's so easy to gravitate towards solutions and strategies that we know we can control like large group programming.

This reminds me of the story of Peter, Jesus, and the boat in Matthew 14:22-33. In this passage Jesus asks Peter to step out of the boat and come to Him. Peter has to leave the safety of his control in order to answer the call of his Lord. I think, "this is us" sometimes: we like to focus on what we can control, what we can pull off, what we can do in terms of KidMin programming—which doesn't always equate to child discipleship. We have to make a similar shift to prioritize child discipleship so that future generations of children and students can experience the love of Jesus and respond to the invitation of the gospel.

Just for a moment, let's set all of our programming aside, and ask the question, what would a "Kid-Focused Philosophy" look like? Let's take another look at the Resilient Child Discipleship definition:

Resilient Child Discipleship

The process of a Christ-follower committing meaningful, intentional, and consistent time and space to a child or a group of children so that they may know who Jesus is and are known by a body of believers (Belong), to place their faith in Jesus and apply the Word of God (Believe), and to reproduce their own discipleship (Become) so that a third spiritual generation can lead and love like Jesus Christ.

What do you see there? We see the presence of loving, caring adults who are being intentional and faithful in engaging children. During their time together, these Christlike adults engage relationally so that these children feel known, loved, cared for. The kids are hearing and experiencing God's Word. They have space to think about it and ask questions. They can explore it, learn it, memorize it and live it out. And we see kids being shown how to engage the culture and live outside of the simulation of "weekend church," loving and leading like Jesus. We call this Belong, Believe and Become—an effective child focused discipleship philosophy—also known as 3B.

Notice what is not there—curriculum, videos, programming, a polished and highly produced experience, etc. The metrics for child discipleship are not measured by these things. They are simply methods or tools for engaging these children. Not that you shouldn't do those things! It's that we didn't start by listing out the programmatic practices first. We started by fleshing out a kid-focused philosophy that's designed to influence discipleship for a lifetime.

Our temptation as KidMin leaders is to go right to the programmatic practices or to put all of our energy into making the existing system better. But as the research is showing, we really don't even know if the existing system is producing long-term discipleship results. (Remember, according to the Barna Group, our best efforts up to this point have only produced 10% resilient disciples). We know we are good at programming, but we don't know what the programming is producing long-term.

KidMin leaders, let's develop a proven, child-focused discipleship philosophy first. Then we will build a system and a program to match the philosophy.

Match the System to the Philosophy

True confession—I'm a systems guy. My team members call me "the engineer." I lead a team of 10 that has to produce an entire ecosystem of resources for church leaders each year. We have writers, designers, editors, artists and project management. We hustle, we pray, we have fun, and we work our system. Without it, it would be an absolute train wreck.

As it relates to local church kid's ministry, systems are very important! Marketing expert Seth Godin says, "It's not (exciting) to talk about building or maintaining an infrastructure, but just try to change the world without one."[5] Infrastructure. Systems. Processes. They are all vitally important. You and I could not meet up at the local Starbucks were it not for systems, processes and infrastructure.

But what system are we talking about? Are we talking about the systems of the past? Systems of the present? Or the systems we need to build the disciples who will lead the church of 2050?

Let's imagine for a moment that all of our church programming and calendar existed on a backup server and all the backups were erased. It crashed. It's gone. Now what? What would we do? Would we start over? If we started over, how would we build our ministry today? Would we raise millions of dollars and build a state-of-the-art education wing? Would you launch an innovative ed-tech learning environment where kids and leaders could access the community from any place on the planet at any time? What if we didn't start with our assumptions about the needs of the system (existing programming), but rather we started with the needs of the child?

What if our ministry started with that young boy or girl looking up at us and asking, *"Where are we going?"*

We need to shift away from the assumed systems of the past, to child-centric thinking for the future of children's ministry to thrive. This will require us as leaders to be learners, observers, listeners and researchers. We must go native with the children in our ministry and in order to do that, we may have to become children ourselves again. Learn how to laugh, play in the physical or digital sandboxes, and little by little, get closer to the needs of a child. Every child, has a need to be known, seen and understood. For our ministries to elevate effective Child Discipleship means that our teams (volunteers, staff, child disciplemakers, etc.) have to personally know the kids in our ministries. What does school look like for them? What is their family life like? What hardships are they facing? As an example, no child should ever be a name on a nametag that gets verified as they leave. Left to itself, that's church efficiency and not the beauty of child discipleship. Again, it's not that the system is wrong (we need a check-in system!), it's that we need to keep the system in perspective. The system is there to match our philosophy, not the philosophy adapting to the system of the past.

IT'S NOT EXCITING TO TALK ABOUT BUILDING OR MAINTAINING AN INFRASTRUCTURE, BUT JUST TRY TO CHANGE THE WORLD WITHOUT ONE

So let's continue this robust conversation on the long-term effectiveness of what we are doing in our children's ministries. We've narrowed our focus to prioritizing our time to "help every child love Jesus for the rest of his or her life" and we aim to accomplish this through "the process of a child believing in, belonging to and becoming like Jesus." Now that we've hit this point, there are a few meaningful questions we can ask:

MEANINGFUL QUESTIONS

- *How can we help every child to have a sense of belonging in our faith community?*
- *Do the kids in our care feel known, loved, seen, heard and engaged?*
- *How can we be a safe haven for kids who come from challenging homes?*
- *Are our "believing" tactics solid enough in a post-Christian culture?*
- *In a time of increased confusion, do our kids understand the basics of the gospel?*
- *Are the kids in our care Bible literate? Do they understand universal truth in a postmodern world?*
- *How can we help kids live outside the simulation of Sunday morning and become like Jesus?*
- *How can we redesign our system to major on the majors that are going to yield the best lifelong fruit?*
- *Is our children's ministry designed to help prepare kids to thrive in their faith in the year 2050?*
- *In the distant future, will the kids in our ministry today "thank us" for preparing them for a future that may be hostile to the Christian faith?*

These are just icebreakers. We think your team has the best questions!

The future we are facing as a faith community may be one where the ways of Jesus are squeezed to the margins. As we face this unknown future together, let's be sure to not start with our preconceived ideas and assumptions about our system and our church programming that may not produce the needed discipleship of the future. Rather, let's start with a compelling "why," a kid-focused philosophy of discipleship and build a system to match. With this direction, we can inspire a entire movement of fully engaged child disciple makers.

Inspire Fully Engaged Child Disciple Makers

The seismic shifts in our culture we discussed at the beginning of this book, although painful, are no surprise. These shifts have resulted in an epidemic of isolation in North America that is overwhelming: fatherlessness, abandonment, divorce, device addiction, neglect, opioid crisis, financial crisis. We could go on. The effects of these epidemics on children are unprecedented—perhaps the most significant crisis of our time. Yet, we are reminded of this hope:

One loving, caring adult engaged in the life of a child can dramatically increase a child's long-term probability for success.

I remember when my daughter and I walked out of church and I asked her about her time at kids' church. She said, "Dad, I don't want to go there anymore?" What? What happened? Immediately, I began interrogating her. She said, "Dad, next week take a look—nobody smiles." WOW! That floored me. Sure enough, we went back the next week and not a single leader was smiling. Everyone was efficient and performing his or her job well, but there was no joy or passion. There was no life. It was as if this ministry was breathing, but wasn't alive.

I've heard these same types of stories as I connect with church leaders and facilitate roundtable discussions nationwide. As a community, we face our own crisis—volunteers. So much of what we do is through the minds, hearts, hands and feet of volunteers. Because of this we are so incredibly thankful for those who serve on our teams! Yet, as KidMin leaders and pastors, Jesus words weigh heavy on our hearts when he said, "The harvest is plentiful but the workers are few." (Matthew 9:37, NIV). We cry out, "May it not be so!" But far too often it is.

And this is precisely what we learned from you in our 2019 research as well:

- *When asked, "Specifically, why don't you view your children's ministry as more successful?" the leading response was "lack of volunteers" as 38.6% of the respondents gave this as their top response.*

- *When asked, "Specifically, why do you view your children's ministry so successfully?" the second highest response was "volunteers" as 26.7% of the respondents gave this as the number two response.*

- *When asked, "How much do you think each of the following potential challenges/ problems is adversely impacting the children's ministry at your church, if at all?" the leading response was "lack of volunteers/workers" out of 17 options.*

What we heard from you in our research is clear: Loving, caring adults make the difference. Through these loving, caring adults, kids hear the good news of Jesus, they understand what love is, they experience the truth of the Bible and the message of Jesus comes alive.

When you see more success in ministry, it's because volunteers are engaging. When you see less success, it's because fewer loving, caring adults are involved. So if effective disciple making takes a disciple maker, and if as a community the research says that our #1 challenge is "we need more disciple makers" than what are we to do about this conundrum?

We need to cast the 2050 vision.

As I look back on my own local church experience, I remember not only recruiting volunteers, but also at times even begging for volunteers. Perhaps you've been there? I found myself thinking, "A volunteer has a role to fill, but a child disciple maker has a calling. How can we get more disciple makers?" We need to cast the 2050 vision. What if they heard the Bernie Sanders and Russell Vought story? What if they knew they were carriers of fire to the next generation? What if they fully knew the power that just one loving, caring adult could have on the long-term development of a child? Part of the rub that we experience as KidMin leaders, is that our programming puts us in a "week-to-week" mentality, but child discipleship is about the long game. We need to cast a new vision for resilient child disciple makers that moves our mindset into our new reality.

As we move toward the year 2050, what will happen if we change nothing? Volunteers will rotate in and rotate out spending time fighting against the constraints of a busy life with short-lived commitments. Might I suggest that being a child disciple maker may cause us to embrace a more selfless culture in the children's wing? This won't be easy, but for future generations to thrive in a modern-day Babylon, it's going to take a different kind of discipleship resilience. One that will gather fully-engaged child disciple makers. We need to cast a better, long-view vision.

Ensure Every Child's Unique Discipleship Pathway

I love sitting in church and watching the screen as the numbers from the nursery appear in front of everyone. XY345C? Whew! That's not my kid and I don't have to perform the walk of shame out of the worship center. We use this "number system method" for privacy, security and anonymity, but in a culture of systems, I do sometimes wonder if we can be about numbers over names? I wonder if our systems of efficiency will be enough to see children as they are where we need to meet them, and then journey with them where they need to go.

Your heart as a leader knows that behind each number is a name, a family, a story of beauty, pain and the promises of God's love for them. Just as Jesus not only taught the masses, He also discipled the twelve, He mentored the few and He had one on one encounters with individuals. He knew people on a personal level. So as we prepare today's kids to lead the church of 2050, what if we designed a new system that put each child on his or her own unique discipleship pathway? How would we do this? Where would we start? I'd like to think that we could start by imagining we are children and we lock eyes with Jesus and He calls us by name.

Know their Names

Most KidMin leaders have this nailed! It's so basic. The sweetest and most life-giving thing said in any language is to hear your name spoken back to you. Do we know the names of our kids? Does your team know their names? Names matter in Scripture and if we are going to get closer to the children in our ministries, we need to get beyond acquaintances and commit their names to memory.

> *Idea: Make sure every single kid in your children's ministry is prayed for, by name, weekly!*

Know their Heart

Isn't it fascinating when we take enough time to sit with a child, how much they can open up. When we do this, we often discover their passions and plans for the world. They allow us to gain access to the deepest and most intimate parts of their soul when we do the simple work of building friendships with kids. I have found that almost every kid has something deep down in their heart that is a driving force within them. It causes them to keep moving and engaging. What is that for the children in your ministry?

> *Idea: Have your volunteers ask the children in your ministry to help you solve a problem. See what kinds of solutions that they come up with. You'll find that they gave you a glimmer into what's going on in their hearts. AND, they will feel a greater sense of belonging and purpose as viable and active participants of your church community.*

Know their Pain and Struggle

Children can live in a basement of emotional pain. It's scary. It's dark. It can cause them great anxiety, fear and even depression. Are we pain sensitive to the children in our ministries, aware and caring, or are we just skimming the surfaces of their lives? I think Jesus went to the parties and hung out with the sinners in order to close the distance between Himself and the pain that resided in each person at those gatherings. Get closer to your kids. Love is the key that unlocks the door to the basement of every child's pain. As we do this, we also discover their struggles. Their struggle is just a superpower in disguise. Their present struggle has the potential to become their future superpower. As we previously mentioned, the Awana leadership team is a perfect example of this. Sitting around a table sharing our childhoods one day, we realized that we were all broken as children. Little did we know that the things we were experiencing were the gymnasiums of life where God saw fit to do some of His best work! What are your kids struggling with? Do you assume they are thriving, just scratching the surface of their realities, or do you and your team care deeply enough to enter and share their pain?

> *Idea: One of the ways to get to know the pain and struggle of children is to express the challenges you have faced as well. Help them know that they are not alone in this world. That being human is something that everyone experiences. When a child sees an adult struggle, they will find that they are not alone in this world and will develop a more lasting connection with the church for years to come.*

Know their Spiritual Growth and Journey

Can you imagine an educational system that didn't track the math, science, grammar and artistic growth and progress of children? It's unthinkable! Yet, in the church, we have very few markers of spiritual growth. In our 2019 research, it became apparent that very few churches are tracking the spiritual growth of children. In our qualitative focus groups, one person said, "Haven't consistently figured out a way to qualitatively measure or track success over the long run." Another person said, "You can't track something as intangible as spiritual growth." But is that true? Is it really true that there is no way to track the spiritual growth of a child? We happen to think that you can track the spiritual growth of a child. It just takes a different mindset, a clear vision of child discipleship and a system to measure and track key indicators of spiritual fruit.

> *Idea: Develop a mind map for belonging, believing and becoming in your child discipleship ministry. Use this as a process to come up with the very best 2 – 3 ideas within each of the 3B areas that you can begin to track for the kids in your ministry. What if you focused on tracking these for 2–3 years? How would this change how you evaluate the effectiveness of your ministry? You may find that some areas are really working–and can then find a way to further maximize those areas. Or, you may find out that some things you are doing are less fruitful, and can revise.*

Believe in their Potential

As you look into every life in your ministry you see beyond the wrinkled clothes, braces and mismatched socks. Train your team to look for each child's full potential: to believe in whom God created them to become. As your team becomes their #1 fan that screams loud from the sidelines of their life, they are building a spiritual legacy that will last for generations.

> *Hint: Give each child in your ministry a word that was uniquely selected for them; Leader, Sunshine, Thinker, Everyone's Friend, Helper, Comedian, Eager Learner, the possibilities are so vast! Explain why this word was selected and encourage them throughout the year to keep pressing forward to become a disciple of Jesus Christ rather than a spectator or participant in the program.*

So, what shifts do you need to make in your ministry?

Are you trying really hard to make the existing system better or more efficient? Or, could you slow down. See the children that God has brought you and seek to make it more relational than ever before?

Child discipleship sees each kid as being on a path to becoming all whom God intends for him or her to be in His Kingdom. Each child is known, loved, understood and has a pathway to spiritual growth as they believe in, belong to and become like Jesus.

Break the Huddle

Earlier on in ministry, I remember meeting a boys' small group on the first night of a new ministry year. They were all over the place. Some were engaged while others were lost in the fields of their own imaginations. I remember that I had one boy say, "So where are we going Mr. Chris?" This is an excellent question. I gathered my boys together and said, "Huddle up! Everyone locks arms. Make no mistake gentlemen, I'm here to disciple you and do everything in my power and ability to help you as you become disciples of Jesus Christ. This is the intention behind everything that I do. It's why I am here. I'm not here to be cool or just be a friend that quietly or apathetically passes through your life. I'm here to be present. To be around. To be reachable. To be an image of Christ for you to follow. This is my commitment to you!"

It got really quiet and my boys looked at my eyes like I've never seen a child or student do before. Finally, they had met someone who was ready to take them on a journey, someone who would take them someplace beyond the routine of KidMin systems. If we are not clear, visionary and specific, KidMin can become merely week-to-week programming. In setting and meeting our short-term goals we may completely miss the ultimate goal of child discipleship. As we prayerfully anticipate the church of 2050, let's unite as a KidMin community around what will shape the fearless future of the church —child discipleship.

This reimagined church is a church made up of child disciple makers. These are the fire carriers. The loving, caring adults who make up an engaging church community who throw their doors and arms open to the children of our families and communities. This is a place of belonging where kids can believe in and become like Jesus. This is the church of 2050.

ESSENTIAL QUESTIONS:

Does your team have a clearly defined vision and mission?

Does this (question above) include a child discipleship pathway for each child in your ministry?

Thinking as an essentialist, what are a few things you should consider stopping or pausing to create more time and space for effective child discipleship?

Do you have a way to measure the effectiveness of your child discipleship ministry? What would be your key markers of success? Have you led your team in this discussion?

The Science of Resilience:
IT'S GOOD NEWS!

CHAPTER 9

Why Did You Leave?

Recently, someone gave me (Valerie) a picture that touched me. A dark-haired, muscular young teenager dressed in *Awana Games* gear smiles out at me. It looks like the picture is circa 1960 something. No one knew it at the time this picture was taken, but in a few years that young boy would become a world-famous comedian, one of the seven original cast members of *Saturday Night Live*. We were introduced to his raucous humor in *Animal House*, and the cult classic, *The Blues Brothers*. That teenager smiling out from the picture was John Belushi.

He also was a member of my high school graduation class. Strangely, for all these years I never knew he had an Awana connection until that picture was given to me. Where was I?

It makes me incredibly sad to think how close he came to belonging, believing and becoming, knowing and loving Jesus for the rest of his life. Instead, tragically, he died in his early thirties of a drug overdose. It could have been so different than it ended up being.

What a great loss. What a great heartbreak.

John, why did you leave? What happened to you?

Who hasn't asked that question over someone?
Why did you leave?

However, if we turn that question around and ask people who had every reason to leave, *"Why did you stay?"* we might understand what contributes to spiritual resilience in people.

IF WE TURN THAT QUESTION AROUND AND ASK PEOPLE WHO HAD EVERY REASON TO LEAVE, "WHY DID YOU STAY?" WE MIGHT UNDERSTAND WHAT CONTRIBUTES TO SPIRITUAL RESILIENCE IN PEOPLE.

"I'VE HEARD IT SAID, 'IT IS THE CHILDREN THE WORLD ALMOST DESTROYS WHO RISE UP TO SAVE IT.'"

Why Did You Stay?

Dr. Wess Stafford is the President emeritus of Compassion International. As a child he was raised in Cote d'Ivoire where his parents served as missionaries. He was enrolled in a boarding school for missionary children he calls Bandulo Christian Academy. For nine months the children attending Bandulo were separated from their parents and families. What no one knew was that Bandulo was a place of rigid control and fearsome consequences. Beatings, abuse of the most humiliating kind, and constant terror were daily life for these vulnerable missionary kids.

Life at Bandulo was horrendous. For a child, it was nearly hellacious. Wess experienced all of that as a boy.

So why did Wess Stafford stay? Why, in light of his suffering, didn't he just chuck his faith? He had every reason to reject Christianity and leave. Many of the children of Bandulo did give up on God. In Wess' words they "fell down and never got up." Instead, Wess became one of the world's most impassioned Christian advocates for children.

These are his words:

"I've heard it said, 'It is the children the world almost destroys who rise up to save it.' I am one of those little ones who was almost destroyed. Many of my childhood friends who suffered the evil of abuse with me fell down in the middle of that nightmare and never got up. After people read my story of experiencing abuse as a child in *Too Small to Ignore*, I am often asked, 'How did you get back up? Why didn't you give up on God and your faith? What made you dedicate your life to Him and to saving children who suffer poverty, abuse, hopelessness?'

"All I can say is, I am simply a product of God's grace. As damaged as I was, I am humbled that God chose to use me. Believe me, if He can still use me, He can redeem and use anyone!

"Looking back, I now realize that as a boy, I chose my belonging. I determined that I belonged not with the cruel and sadistic boarding school, but rather, within the bosom of a loving African village, and nestled within a caring family.

"My believing was also a choice. I chose to reject the beliefs of my oppressors. Their faith lived out in cruelty to us children did not match what I understood and believed to be true—that our heavenly Father loved us little children and welcomed us into His arms and into His kingdom.

"My becoming was not understood by me as a child. But my hurt and sorrow shaped my heart and directed my path toward a lifelong battle against poverty (in my African village) and abuse (in my boarding school). That very anger and pain fueled my passion to fight back with the rest of my life. I am so grateful God led me to Compassion International, a very powerful tool in my calling and mission.

"People tell me they are in awe of that resilience. How could I forgive, pick myself up and enter a lifelong fight on behalf of other hurting children? Looking back, I can trace His orchestrations along my path, and above all, I see His amazing grace. I belong to Him. I believe in Him. I strive to live my life becoming more like Him. What is redemption if not rescued souls ... belonging, believing and becoming?"

Resilience. Sometimes it is forged in a child's life while he or she is suffering some of life's cruelest challenges. But God has mercy on us and responds to our suffering. At the very point where we are broken, abused and humiliated, God makes us strong. God converted the anger and pain of Wess Stafford's childhood into a passion to fight for children who can't fight for themselves.

That's resilience.

The Science of Resilience: Why Kids Get Back Up

Why is it that some kids experience adverse conditions, yet they get back up? Child discipleship can play a significant role in this process of "getting back up." Child discipleship that's built on belonging, believing and becoming develops resilience in kids.

While researching for this book, specifically while studying the "science of resilience" in children, I (Matt) posted a comment on social media pertaining to resilient kids. I promptly received a direct message from a friend (you know who you are :) who shared, "kids are not resilient." Thanks to the plethora of research available on the science of resilience, I was able to kindly reply, "That's not what the science says."

You may be surprised or even frightened by all that pops up when you google the phrase "the science of..." But if you scroll down far enough you will come across "the science of resilience." This area of study has been of increasing interest in recent years. But why? In short, it's a seismic need. Marketplace employers, educators, physicians, therapists, researchers, coaches, parents and beyond–have observed a significant need for resilience to be developed in young people. It is important to learn not simply to cope with life's adversities, but to learn to thrive into adulthood. Curious? We have been too.

This science comes with good news! Resilience can be developed. It can be developed in adults, and it can be developed in children. But what is resilience according to the experts? The American Psychological Association defines resilience as "the process of adapting well in the face of adversity, trauma, tragedy and threat..." [1] These negative experiences in children are often referred to as Adverse Childhood Experiences (ACE). As we think about the future of the church, one that may be increasingly marginalized by secular culture, this science (what we can learn and apply to children in adverse conditions) should be of significant interest as we prepare today's kids to live, lead and thrive in a very different future. So how can we help them develop resilience?

In *Resilience: The Science of Mastering Life's Greatest Challenges*, authors Steven M. Southwick and Dennis S. Charney interviewed Vietnam POWs, and other remarkably resilient people, looking for common characteristics that they shared.

They interviewed people like Jerry White, who lost his leg in a landmine while hiking as a college student and struggled afterwards with depression. In the following years, he founded Landmine Survivors Network, which was awarded the Nobel Peace Prize in 1997. Jerry not only survived, he thrived and excelled. [2]

That's resilience.

They interviewed others like Elizabeth Ebaugh, who was kidnapped, raped and thrown over a bridge into a freezing river to die. She survived and lived to build a thriving clinical social work practice that focuses on helping survivors of trauma and tragedy. Elizabeth not only survived, she thrived and excelled. [3]

That's resilience.

During their interviews with resilient people they noticed shared emerging factors—that contribute to resilience. These are the 10 resilience factors they found through their interview process: [4]

Ten resilience factors found in the interview process:

Fostering optimism

Facing fear

Solidifying moral compass

Practicing religion and spirituality

Attracting and giving social support

Imitating resilient role models

Physical training

Mental and emotional training

Enhancing cognitive and emotional flexibility

Finding meaning, purpose and growth [2]

As our team reflected on this list, we observed that many of these items are *relational* in nature. Just look at how some of the items on this list above would be *applied* and *implemented* in the life of a child:

What we see in the Resilience Factors:

A moral compass is formed by a worldview shared through a **community**.

Spirituality and religion are formed by faith **communities** and **key individuals**.

Social support comes from **people**.

Role models are often **coaches**, **mentors**, **family** members and **members of our community**.

Training frequently transacts from **person** to **person**.

There's a clear theme here. Resilience is formed by a combination of the internal makeup of an individual in collision with external adverse experiences. The catalyst, however, to the development of resilience is often times an additional person who extends belonging and relationship for one facing adversity.

In an article titled, *INBRIEF: The Science of Resilience,* the Center on the Developing Child of Harvard University says that, "Resilience requires supportive relationships and opportunities for skill building. **No matter the source of hardship, the single most common factor for children who end up doing well is having the support of at least one stable and committed relationship with a parent, caregiver or other adult.** These relationships are the active ingredient in building resilience: they provide the personalized responsiveness, scaffolding, and protection that can buffer children from developmental disruption." [5]

One of the first psychologists to study resilience, Emily Warner, followed the lives of children raised in impoverished homes by alcoholic, abusive, or mentally ill parents. Werner observed that resilient children—the ones who grew up to be emotionally healthy adults—found at least one person who truly supported them and served as an admired role model. [6]

So what is this recurring theme? It's a fire carrier. It's the presence of a loving, caring adult. It's "but there was a church." This is the power of belonging. **The KidMin soil that prioritizes the essential component of belonging is a garden where believing and becoming can grow, flourish and thrive.** Today's kids—now more than ever—need a community of belonging to help them develop the type of navigational resilience they will need to thrive in their faith in an uncertain future.

As advocates for the gospel and child disciple makers, what we want more than anything is for our kids to "be there" in the kingdom of heaven. I sometimes envision looking across the vast multitude of God's people worshiping King Jesus in heaven, catching the joy and adoration on the faces of my two sons—what more could we want?! Until then we pray for our kids who are facing a unique future. Until then we can learn from the science of resilience and build a church community that extends the love of Jesus to today's kids like never before. Let's inspire and equip our volunteer teams with this critical information. Through walking in relationship with you and your volunteer team, kids can navigate truly unique times as you lead them to believe in the gospel of Christ and become more like Jesus in a world in need of His hope and salvation.

> AT RESILIENT CHILDREN— THE ONES WHO GREW UP TO BE EMOTIONALLY HEALTHY ADULTS— FOUND AT LEAST ONE PERSON WHO TRULY SUPPORTED THEM AND SERVED AS AN ADMIRED ROLE MODEL.

All But Normal

We shared Shawn Thornton's story earlier of growing up in a home where his mother suffered from Traumatic Brain Injury—TBI. His childhood was chaotic, unpredictable and emotionally explosive. Like Wess Stafford, Shawn Thornton is also resilient.

We asked Shawn, Senior Pastor at well-known Calvary Community Church in Westlake Village, California, "Why did you stay? Why did you stick with your faith after such a difficult childhood?"

These are his words:

"After some of my longest and dearest friends read my memoir, *All But Normal: Life on Victory Road,* they ask me a simple question. "So, why didn't you or your brother walk away from the church or even your faith?" I get it. If things seemed so difficult and challenging during my formative years, why, when I grew up, did I not simply run as far away as possible from anything resembling Christianity? There are three things I have identified over the last couple of years that provided the right atmosphere and oxygen for me when life's circumstances were suffocating my childhood. These three were critical to my belonging, believing, and becoming.

"**First**, what I saw in terms of my parents' hearts over time impacted my view of true Christian faith. In their brokenness, my parents both pursued knowing, loving and serving Jesus. While there were many adverse events, hurtful words, and deeply discouraging moments that were a part of our home, my brother and I witnessed a clear trajectory of growth, faith and a genuine desire to be used by God to help others. Looking back at my years growing up, I realize that my brother and I (even as kids) focused less on all of the negative things that happened and more on the journey, the trajectory of our parents' lives. They were honest in the struggle AND honest in their seeking God more. That made an impact!

"The **second** major factor that encouraged me to hold to my faith was the genuineness of our local church fellowship. Twin Branch Bible Church in Mishawaka, Indiana, never had an attendance higher than 350 people. Most of my years growing up there, the church averaged about 200 people on Sundays.

Like what I had seen in the heart of my parents, God allowed me to look beyond the flaws and failures of the people of Twin Branch Bible Church and see a caring family that eagerly included me.

"Most of the folks in our church knew little or nothing about my mother's disturbing and disruptive outbursts or behavior. That did not matter. They were themselves. They were sincere and faithful in their love for me. The people of Twin Branch created an imperfect, but healthy, family environment in which I always felt known, loved and valued. The dear folks within our church let me be me. They even allowed me to experiment in serving the Lord without any fear that they would sideline or condemn me. Whether it was Sunday school, Awana, youth group, or some other ministry, caring and kind adults spoke into my life in Jesus' name. They embraced me without judgment of my family or me.

"Besides the trajectory of my parents' lives and the incredible local church environment in which I was raised, there was a **third** factor that kept me from walking away from Christianity. It's how God Himself met me in some of the darkest moments of my life and our home. While I never heard a voice, had a dream with Jesus in it or saw an angel covered in a heavenly glow, I know God met me. There were distinct moments when God filled my aching heart with His healing and peace. He reassured my mind that I was indeed His, and He would walk with me through the deepest challenges in my life. Over the years, I have struggled to describe adequately how God met me when I was a scared little boy, a middle school kid who couldn't stop crying, or a high school student who felt like he didn't belong anywhere.

> "Belonging, believing and becoming, for me, all rest on the trajectory of my parents' hearts, the environment of a loving local church, and God meeting me in moments of deep personal pain. I guess it seems an odd thing to say that in all of the craziness of my childhood, I never considered walking away from my faith, Christianity or the ministry.

"God blessed me with a childhood I would not have chosen for myself. He did that so I, as a pastor, would understand how hard it is for people to feel like they belong, to believe God and what He says and to become what God has called them to be—like Jesus."

RESILIENCE CAN BE DEVELOPED, AND YOU AND YOUR TEAM CAN DISCIPLE CHILDREN AND STUDENTS TO ENGAGE THE CULTURE AND LEAD THE CHURCH.

Foundation for Resilience

Belong, Believe and Become were the foundation for spiritual resilience in both Shawn Thornton's and Wess Stafford's lives. Within the nurturing communities of faith, exposed to the sometimes messy faiths of others, they developed spiritual resilience that not only helped them survive, but gave them incredible strength to excel and thrive in Christ. Resilience can be developed, and you and your team can disciple children and students to engage the culture and lead the church.

The opportunity we have to welcome today's kids (who face a variety of adverse conditions) to belong in relationship to us as child and youth disciple makers is remarkable. As their eyes gaze across the horizon of the broken world around them, may they be captivated by the radiance of the church. May they gasp at her remarkable beauty and say, "I've found my people!."

In the next chapter, we are going to explore in greater detail the power of belong, believe, become found in the Resilient Child Discipleship Philosophy. We will define some terms, share some stories, unpack the biblical basis and dig into some research. Let's go!!!

ESSENTIAL QUESTIONS:

Have you asked the young adults who have left your church, "why did you leave?" For those who stayed, have you asked them, "why did you stay?"

What can your team learn from the science of resilience? How can you apply what you are learning to help the volunteers and kids in your ministry?

What if we equipped our local church volunteers with the "science of resilience" information? Can you see this information inspiring your volunteers to greater levels of empathy and engagement with the kids in your children's ministry?

Resilient Child Discipleship:
IT'S ALL ABOUT BELONG, BELIEVE AND BECOME

CHAPTER 10

NASA was founded in 1958 and like many organizations in their early days, it was struggling to find its way.

By the early 1960s, NASA was simply floundering. In spite of their significant expectations and an approximate budget of $80 billion a year, NASA lacked focus.[1] Their culture was laden with bureaucracy and too many competing priorities. The Soviet Union, on the other hand, was making swift progress and was beginning to win the "space race" of the 1960s.

With the eyes of the American public looking to them with great imagination and anticipation, NASA set out with high hopes and big dreams. Their objectives were outstanding:

The expansion of human knowledge of phenomena in the atmosphere and space.

The preservation of the role of the United States as the leader in aeronautical and space science and technology and in the application thereof to the conduct of peaceful activities within and outside the atmosphere.

The preservation of the United States preeminent position in aeronautics and space through research and technology development related to associated manufacturing processes. [2]

But wait, there's more: the objectives listed above are just three of NASA's eight main objectives. See the problem? Their systemic problem was what all too many organizations struggle with—lack of focus. Don't get me wrong, these are noble objectives. Yet, the eight objectives were dividing the organization's capacity. Too many objectives made it nearly impossible to focus and make progress toward a clearly defined target. All of that began to change though in 1961.

In 1961, President John F. Kennedy made the pronouncement to NASA, "Land a man on the moon and return him safely to the earth before this decade is out." With this clear and specific objective by our nation's President, NASA's strategy went from that of diversified energies, to a singular focus of energy with the aim of significant impact. Suddenly, NASA's strategy went from broad to narrow. Get to the moon. Land a man on the moon. Get him home safely. Do this by the end of 1969. Check.

But what was it going to take to do this? In order to accomplish this very focused mission, NASA leaders had to solve three problems: propulsion, navigation, and human life support.

 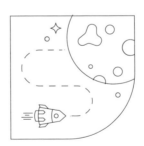 

PROPULSION

Get the Apollo out of the earth's atmosphere and back to earth.

NAVIGATION

Help the Apollo steer in the right direction when needed.

LIFE SUPPORT

Maintain the health and safety of the astronauts with the resources available on the spacecraft.

Suddenly, everything changed! NASA rallied around these three core problems with remarkable focus. Teams were formed. Objectives were clarified. Problems were identified. Processes and systems were put in place. New technologies were innovated and BAM! On July 20, 1969, the nation watched in awe as Neil Armstrong stepped on the moon's surface and spoke these unforgettable words:

"That's one small step for man. And one giant leap for mankind."

That's poetry spoken in the theater of our universe.

What seemed nearly unattainable ... what seemed so far off and distant ... almost impossible, it happened!

But it happened because one leader not only had a vision, but declared a specific mission: a mission that was clear, focused and measurable. And the entire organization got behind it and delivered on execution.

In children's ministry, the year 2050 almost feels as distant as the moon. But the culture race is on—big time. Secular culture is designed to distract our kids into corrupt ideology or to lull our children into consumer complacency. What must we do to win in this race and prepare today's kids to engage the culture and lead the church of the future with a fearless, resilient faith? As we discussed in Chapter 8, a clarified mission of Resilient Child Discipleship comes alive through a philosophy known to influence long-term discipleship fruit into adulthood: Belong, Believe and Become.

Defining Resilient Child Discipleship

Having served in local churches (children's ministry, youth ministry) and having led in nonprofit ministries, our leadership can relate to the plight faced by NASA. Specifically within children and youth ministry we can become overwhelmed with a multiplicity of priorities like VBS, Sunday school, youth group, large group, small group, community groups, midweek, staff management, volunteer management, volunteer recruitment, staff and volunteer training, key church relationships, budgeting and planning, business meetings, and the seemingly endless number of special events. Whew! And we were just getting started!

NASA came to the place as an organization where it reevaluated its strategy and chose to stop or pause some activities in order to focus on three specific components to win in the space race. In the same way, as child disciple makers, we need to step back and ask ourselves, "Is our current strategy and philosophy going to nurture and influence resilient disciples who will lead the church in 2050?" If the answer to that question is "yes," then you have likely already worked through a process of evaluating, effective philosophy and key markers that influence long-term fruit. But if the answer is "no," then consider Resilient Child Discipleship based on three focused components that we referenced earlier in the book:

```
Resilient Child Discipleship

The process of a Christ-follower committing meaningful,
intentional, and consistent time and space to a child or a
group of children so that they may know who Jesus is and are
known by a body of believers (Belong), to place their faith
in Jesus and apply the Word of God (Believe), and to reproduce
their own discipleship (Become) so that a third spiritual
generation can lead and love like Jesus Christ.
```

Resilient Child Discipleship doesn't start with programs. It doesn't start with our existing 21st century systems. It starts with a universal curiosity around, what makes child discipleship effective, long-term and fruitful? As church leaders and kid-influencers, we have the unique opportunity to let this curiosity inform our programs and our systems, ultimately resulting in more effective local church, gospel-based ministry.

RESILIENT CHILD DISCIPLESHIP STARTS WITH A UNIVERSAL CURIOSITY AROUND WHAT MAKES CHILD DISCIPLESHIP EFFECTIVE, LONG-TERM AND FRUITFUL.

Three Components of Resilient Child Discipleship: Belong, Believe and Become

Belong, Believe and Become is the foundation for spiritual resilience. From child to child the environments and the variables change, but when these components are present, the probability for long-term discipleship fruit goes up—even in the face of adverse conditions.

As an organization, we got really curious about, "What makes child discipleship effective, long-term and fruitful?" in 2014. At that point, we began studying the Scriptures with specific interest in the life and ministry of Jesus. We also studied existing and accessible data as well as conducted our own research. Our leadership team has facilitated over 1,000 in-person conversations with church leaders gaining their insight and feedback. We even studied our 70-year history as a global children and youth ministry—looking at both the ups and downs of our own successes and failures. We simply wanted to know, what is it that produces long-term discipleship fruit in the lives of kids into their adulthood?

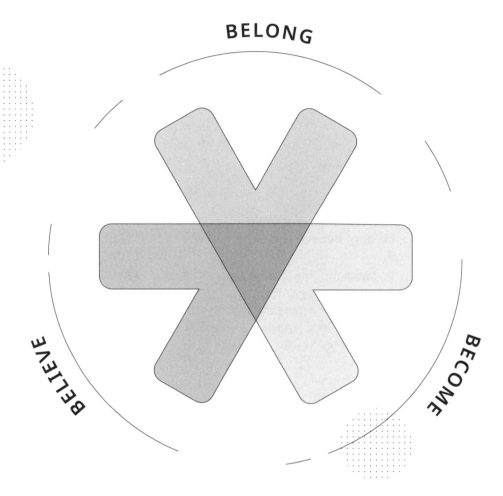

*Belong, Believe, and Become is the
foundation for spiritual resilience.*

All of our learning continued to point to three effective components that make up the Resilient Child Discipleship philosophy: Belong, Believe and Become. Let's define the terms:

 BELONG

Highly relational ministry led by loving and caring adults

 BELIEVE

Deeply Scriptural ministry rooted in the truth of God's Word and the power of the gospel

BECOME

Truly experiential ministry, designed to move kids from simulation to real-world application of faith-based living

Time and time again, these components show up as the central factors to Resilient Child Discipleship that lead to transformation in the lives of children. Our ministry partnerships engage 4.7 million kids in 122 countries. Not a week goes by that we don't receive reports or personal stories of belong, believe and become from our ministry partners like Compassion International, World Vision, missionaries, church planters or pastors from one of our 61,000 global church partners. Even as I have reflected back on my (Matt) own story, I don't have to look too far before I begin to see these same themes emerge.

My parents divorced when I was a young child. My dad was an abusive man and lived a lifetime of hurting those around him, resulting in a wake of damaged relationships. Although my mom had primary custody of my brother and me (which was the best choice), my dad began pushing for joint custody when I was 15. After much consideration as a young man, I ended up deciding that joint custody was not the wisest decision. This decision not to go through with joint child custody made my dad very angry and he told me he didn't want to see me any more.

THEY SIMPLY LOVED ME THROUGH THEIR CONSISTENT PRESENCE.

Wow! Talk about pain and confusion. It was during this season of my life when loving, caring adults like Kimbol and Nancy D., Mike H. and Larry D. stepped in relationally and invested in me. They taught me the Scriptures. They encouraged me. They hung out with me. They identified and named strengths and gifts I didn't even know that I had. They simply loved me through their consistent presence. Throughout this season, they walked beside me at church, in youth group, at community gatherings, in mentoring sessions and even just going out for ice cream. They pointed me in the direction of my life calling and they gave me opportunities to grow, gain experience and lead.

Did you see it? It's right there: *Belong, Believe* and *Become.* It's all over my story. I was at a vulnerable spot when my dad walked out and left me emotionally abandoned, wounded and confused. I could have gone a lot of different directions—certainly anywhere, but the church. But there was a church ... These men and women communicated to me with every fiber of their being that I **belonged**. I knew that they loved me. I could see it in their eyes, feel it in the handwritten cards, in their consistent, relational pursuit and presence. Pastor Kimbol and youth pastor Mike taught me the Scriptures in both formal church opportunities and in informal mentoring times. Deacon Larry would bring Scripture into the conversation as he encouraged me to stay focused on my faith in Jesus and to be careful not to stray toward the broad path that leads to destruction. They were mine and I was theirs. And because of these loving, caring adults, my faith in Jesus was cemented–I **believed**! I saw Christ in them and they helped me see the miracle of the gospel through their teaching of the Word. In addition, they gave me opportunity upon opportunity to serve, volunteer, lead and create. They showed me how to **become** like Jesus and gave me the tools I still carry with me to this very day as I lead and disciple the upcoming generations.

Can you see the components of Resilient Child Discipleship in your story? Can you see where these three components have shaped the children and students in your church community? How about your kids or your grandkids?

But why is it that Belong, Believe and Become—out of all of the possible factors—have so much influence in lifelong discipleship?

In the remaining pages of this chapter we are going to explore responses to that question. We will dig more deeply into why Belong, Believe and Become are the key contributing factors to Resilient Child Discipleship by looking through the lense of: 1. A Biblical Basis, and 2. Noteworthy Research.

— *1*

A BIBLICAL BASIS: BELONG, BELIEVE, BECOME

The Resilient Child Discipleship philosophy of Belong, Believe and Become is deeply rooted in the Scriptures. These words and the intentionality behind them frequently appear throughout the Bible, but often not grouped together as written above. Belong, believe and become is expressed in the books, letters and countless encounters between God and humanity. This discipleship philosophy serves as a biblical and theological roadmap for many to understand the motives, desires and expectations of our Savior and the corresponding and complementary behaviors of humanity. In that, humankind can understand true belonging because Jesus came looking for us (Luke 19:10, John 1:14). That God's desire is for each of us to believe in Him for salvation (2 Peter 3:9, John 20:30-31). Finally, that He desires for each of us to become who we are created to be and fulfill our purpose in carrying out His will for our lives (1 Peter 2:2, Romans 8:28-29, 1 John 3:2).

Belong: A Biblical Basis

In Romans 1:6, Paul greets the church in Rome by saying, "including you who are called to belong to Jesus Christ." The entirety of the Scriptures shouts to the world that we belong to God. In the beginning, humanity was created to be in perfect union with God and belong to Him, for we are His creation (Genesis 1:26). There is an intimacy that was always part of His original design for our relationship with Him. We are His masterpiece and reflect the image of God in this world (Ephesians 2:10). Christ's motivation to bring us back to Himself is the very premise of the incarnation. God came down and entered into the muck and mire of this world. Why? Because we belong to Him.

Humanity was always created to be in intimate proximity to God. It's in that relationship that we know how to love one another (1 John 4:19). As the world will know that we are His disciples by our love for one another (John 13:35). This attitude of love is the essence of true belonging. Jesus desires to make a space at the table for everyone. Men, women and especially children from all walks of life and context have a space to find true belonging in Jesus. Jesus said in Matthew 19, *"Let the little children come to me and do not hinder them, for to such belongs the kingdom of heaven."* From children, which at this point in history, many thought to be the lowest of culture and society, to the woman at the well (John 4) an outcast, to Nicodemus (John 3) the academic and spiritual elite of his time, and Zacchaeus (Luke 19) a conformist unwanted nobody. Each of them finds belonging in Christ.

The biblical account of Jesus' interaction with Zacchaeus (Luke 19:1-10) provides the essential framework of how Christ did ministry relationally. Jesus was passing through Jericho and there was a tiny, little man hanging out in a sycamore tree. You see Zacchaeus fit the mold of a conformist unwanted nobody. He was a tax collector. Like most tax collectors at the time, he took advantage of his position to profit from adding fees beyond the tax desired to be collected. This didn't make him anyone's friend or favorite person. Scripture even captures the consternation of the people. It says, *and when they saw it, they all grumbled, "He has gone in to be the guest of a man who is a sinner."* We all have a great hope to belong because of Jesus interaction with Zacchaeus. Notice what Jesus does in this story. Jesus calls Zacchaeus by name. There's a personal connection that drives the rest of the story. Jesus closed the proximity between Him and Zacchaeus. Jesus says, *"Zacchaeus, hurry and come down, for I must stay at your house today."* Think of all the invites and gatherings that Zacchaeus must have missed because of who he was known to be. Finally, Jesus wants entry into his daily life. There's something very personal about inviting someone into your home. Everything is on display. The good, bad and ugly. It's all there in living color and that's where Jesus wants to be. In the life of Zacchaeus or in our own lives, Jesus knows our name. Jesus wants to close the gap between us and Him, and He wants to gain access to our most intimate spaces. And the beauty of this story is that Zacchaeus was forever changed.

Believe: A Biblical Basis

In John's Gospel, he says, *"Now Jesus did many other signs in the presence of the disciples, which are not written in this book; but these are written so that you may believe that Jesus is the Christ, the Son of God, and that by believing you may have life in His name"* (John 20:30-31). For every man, woman, and child, the primary role of the Gospels is to present the person of Christ with the most considerable amount of evidence possible. No message or movement in all history has had an impact like the gospel of Jesus Christ. In Romans 1:16, Paul says, *"For I am not ashamed of the gospel, for it is the power of God for salvation to everyone who believes, to the Jew first and also to the Greek."* For Christ alone is the only perfectly qualified individual in all of history that can forgive sin and meet all the requirements of His divine standard.

This is also the essence of John 3:16, *For God so loved the world that He gave His one and only Son, that whoever believes in Him should not perish but have eternal life (NIV).*

> *GOD CAME DOWN AND ENTERED INTO THE MUCK AND MIRE OF THIS WORLD. WHY? BECAUSE WE BELONG TO HIM.*

We are reminded of this in many passages of Scripture. The impact of God's Word on those who believe in Him. Acts 6:7 says ... *and the word of God continued to increase, and the number of the disciples multiplied greatly in Jerusalem, and a great many of the priests became obedient to the faith.* This is the power and impact of the Word of God. Hebrews 4:12 reminds us of its power. The writer of Hebrews says, *For the Word of God is living and active, sharper than any two-edged sword, piercing to the division of soul and spirit, of joints and of marrow, and discerning the thoughts and intentions of the heart.*

In Matthew 16, Jesus asks two essential questions of His disciples. Jesus asks, *"Who do people say the Son of Man is?"* They replied, *"Some say John the Baptist; others say Elijah; and still others, Jeremiah or one of the prophets."*

"But what about you?" He asked. *"Who do you say I am?"*

Simon Peter answered, *"You are the Messiah, the Son of the living God."* When it comes to belief, there's the opinion of the crowd that will no doubt influence the perspective of many. However, Jesus makes a b-line to the crux of the issue, for each person must decide on their own if they believe Jesus to be the Messiah, the Son of the living God. As it was with the disciples, so it is for every person. The core outcome of belief is to align and identify oneself with Christ. Belief is all about deeply scriptural ministry rooted in the truth of God's word and in the power of the gospel.

Become: A Biblical Basis

Finally, Paul expresses the idea of becoming to the believers in Corinth. In 2 Corinthians 3:18, Paul says, *"And we all, with unveiled face, beholding the glory of the Lord, are being transformed into the same image from one degree of glory to another. For this comes from the Lord, who is the Spirit."* Paul also expresses a similar idea to the church in Rome. Paul says, *"Do not conform to the pattern of this world, but be transformed by the renewing of your mind. Then you will be able to test and approve what God's will is—His good, pleasing and perfect will* (Romans 12:2, NIV). In the Scriptures, there is an expectation that every believer is in the process of becoming. There is a divine metamorphosis and a transformation that occurs as each experiential moment of our sanctification helps to refine us into a perfect image of Jesus.

That's why Jesus sent His disciples out of the classroom and into the world. The Christian life and every believer's becoming is more than the culmination of countless hours of theory and simulation. It must be balanced by daily practice in the context of reality. The disciples needed to experience it. They needed to see, first hand the power of Christ. Luke 10:1-23 shows us an example of the methodology of Christ. Jesus believed in getting outside of a simulation environment. Jesus sends out seventy-two disciples in pairs of two to each of the places that He was about to go. He gives them specific instructions to guide their habits and behavior. When they returned, they were filled with joy and said, *"Lord, even the demons submit to us in your name."* But, Jesus corrected their observation and amplified their thinking by saying, "He replied, *"I saw Satan fall like lightning from heaven. I have given you authority to trample on snakes and scorpions and to overcome all the power of the enemy; nothing will harm you. However, do not rejoice that the spirits submit to you, but rejoice that your names are written in Heaven (NIV)."* This experience is a valuable teachable moment between the disciples and Jesus. That's how God does some of His best and most memorable work in the lives of people. From the belly of a great fish (Jonah 1:17), to a burning bush (Exodus 3), to the seventy-two disciples being sent out.

Each one of us is in the process of becoming and is the result of countless divine appointments and experiences carefully and masterfully crafted by our Lord (Philippians 2:13).

———

What happens when a person or group of people belong to Jesus, believe in Him, and desire to become all that God has created them to be? You get a church! In Acts 2:42-47, Luke describes the early church and gives us a short but powerful description of the fellowship of believers. He says, *"And they devoted themselves to the apostles' teaching and the fellowship, to the breaking of bread and prayers. And awe came upon every soul, and many wonders and signs were being done through the apostles. And all who believed were together and had all things in common. And they were selling their possessions and belongings and distributing the proceeds to all, as any had need. And day by day, attending the temple together and breaking bread in their homes, they received their food with glad and generous hearts, praising God and having favor with all the people. And the Lord added to their number day by day those who were being saved."*

WE TAKE GREAT COMFORT IN THE UNCHANGING RELIABILITY AND AUTHORITY OF SCRIPTURE.

This passage of Scripture echoes each piece of belong, believe, and become. The early church found belonging in their common bond of Jesus Christ and with each other. They *were together and had all things in common.* Their identities were in Christ and with each other. They found the essence of true belonging as they lived out Paul's similar encouragement to the Philippians in *Do nothing from selfish ambition or conceit, but in humility count others more significant than yourselves* (Philippians 2:3). They gathered together under the banner of common belief in the Apostle's teaching, the words and instructions passed down to them by Jesus Christ. Finally, they became the Church as God added to their number many individuals who were saved and started their own journey of becoming. In this, they fulfilled the purpose that Christ gave to the disciples in Matthew 28:19-20, *Go therefore and make disciples* [Become] *of all nations, baptizing them in the name of the Father and of the Son and of the Holy Spirit, teaching them to observe all that I have commanded you* [Believe]. *And behold, I am with you always, to the end of the age* [Belong].

Cover to cover, the Bible gives examples of these three components (Belong, Believe, and Become) appearing over and over again. From creation to the incarnation and Jesus calling His disciples these themes are evident. From doubting Thomas finding belief only after he had first belonged (relational proximity to Jesus) to Peter, having been reinstated after the grievous sin of denying Christ three times so that he could become the leader of the Church—we can see the foundation of spiritual resilience being formed.

We take great comfort in the unchanging reliability and authority of Scripture. Now let's also take a look at the data and analysis of modern research and how these practical findings can shape our child discipleship philosophy today.

2

NOTEWORTHY RESEARCH:
BELONG, BELIEVE, BECOME

Like you, we are lifetime learners. We love to learn in a variety of ways and one of those ways is research. For pastors and church leaders, research continues to be a key way to learn, gain wisdom and inform the way we navigate in an ever changing culture. We also look to research because it helps us to discern the times. Yet, as important as research is, nothing is more important than our faith, dependency upon Christ, prayer to God and reliance upon the Holy Spirit. So as we approach this next section together, we do so with this clear understanding: we value research because we can learn to gain and apply wisdom to the glory of God.

In his book *Transforming Children into Spiritual Champions* in 2003, George Barna penned these words, "Most families do not have a genuine spiritual life together ... first, they are merely following the precedent that was set for them ... second, most churchgoing parents are neither spiritually mature nor spiritually inclined and, therefore, they do not have a sense of urgency or necessity about raising their kids to be spiritual champions ..."[3] The research behind this project and numerous projects that would follow helped ignite what we now call the modern "family ministry" or "NextGen ministry" movement. Within this overall movement the common message was "Parents are the primary spiritual leaders in the lives of their children. It's the church's job to partner with and equip parents." This is a true message straight from the pages of Deuteronomy 6! Yet, In Dr. Kara Powell and Dr. Chap Clark's research behind their book *StickyFaith* we are reminded that, "Most parents don't talk faith with their kids. 12% of youth have a regular dialogue with their mom or dad on faith issues."[4] Not only are parents struggling at home, they are attending church inconsistently. In a study Awana commissioned in 2019, we discovered that "inconsistent attendance of Kids/Families" is the second most adversely impacted area of local church children's ministry.[5]

So are we making progress? Has the family ministry movement moved the needle? Due to the seismic shifts Valerie discussed earlier in the book, no one seems to be quite sure. As church leaders, we all feel a deep frustration by asking spiritually anemic adults who are barely surviving to lead their kids spiritually. Although it's happening in some of our church families, the "at home" discipleship experience is a small percentage.

So what are we to do? Abandon family ministry? Absolutely not! Abandon church ministry? Never! Resilient discipleship is about changing the way we look at children's, youth and family ministry. The reality is that many parents will never go along on the discipleship journey. These parents are spiritually anemic, distracted, broken, wounded or perhaps not even a Christ-follower. So what are we supposed to do as church leaders and child-influencers? We must have a "belong, believe, become" strategy for every child ... the child with healthy, thriving Christ-following parents, and the child with little to no parental, spiritual engagement.

Christian Smith and Patricia Snell zero in on this idea when they say, "... no single factor can produce high levels of emerging adult religiousness. Instead, multiple combinations of factors working together are necessary to more likely than not produce that outcome. When teenagers' lives reflect only one strong factor, their chances of becoming highly religious emerging adults are lower than average." They continue, "... every most-likely path to highly religious emerging adulthood must include combinations of distinctly different kinds of causal factors, almost always including groupings of relational, personal subjective, and devotional practice factors. In almost all cases, necessary among these variables are:

> *Strong, personal **relationships** with adults who bond teenagers to faith communities (either parents or supportive non-parents),*

> *Strong expressions of subjective teen personal faith commitment and **experience** (high importance of faith, few doubts, many religious experiences), and*

> *High frequencies of religious practice: prayer and **Scripture reading**."* [6]

Smith and Snell are hitting on the resilient discipleship core thesis. Resilient Child Discipleship is not about a single factor. Resilient Child Discipleship is about a combination of factors working together. As they reference above, "relationships" (belonging), "experience" (becoming) and "Scripture reading" (believing). For the churched kids, for the non-churched kids, for the kids with highly engaged parents and for the kids who live in parental neglected homes, as KidMin and youth leaders, we need a combination of distinctly different factors that work together to forge effective discipleship.

We are hopeful about children's, youth and family ministry, because **research supports that resilient child disciple making is possible.** The church can do this! The combination of factors are doable and achievable. Let's take a brief look at the supporting research.

---

*Note: We are only publishing a fraction of the research we collected for the sake of brevity Please visit **ResilientDisciples.com** for additional free resources and information.*

Belong Research

In her book *Daring Greatly,* Dr. Brené Brown speaks of the importance of belonging. "I define belonging as the innate human desire to be part of something larger than us. One of the biggest surprises in this research was learning that fitting in and belonging are not the same thing. In fact, fitting in is one of the greatest barriers to belonging. Fitting in is about assessing a situation and becoming who you need to be in order to be accepted. Belonging, on the other hand, doesn't require us to change who we are; it requires us to be who we are." She goes on to say, "When I asked a large group of eighth-graders to break into small teams and come up with the differences between fitting in and belonging, their answers floored me: Belonging is being somewhere you want to be, and they want you. Fitting in is being somewhere you really want to be, but they don't care one way or the other. Belonging is being accepted for you. Fitting in is being accepted for being like everyone else. I get to be me if I belong. I have to be like you to fit in." [7]

One of the deepest longings of the human heart is to know, "Where do I belong? Who are my people?" As God's people, we know that the central story of the Bible is of His love for us. God sent His Son, Jesus Christ, who came to redeem us and bring us into His kingdom to find true belonging. This is the mission of the church. This is you!

As local church leaders and child and student influencers, check out some of these findings on the power of belonging:

The Belonging Church:

Being the Church Makes a Difference
"By far, the number one way that churches made the teens in our survey feel welcomed and valued was when adults in the congregation showed an interest in them." [8]

Church Attendance Matters
"The closest our research has come to that definitive silver bullet is this sticky finding: for high school and college students, there is a relationship between attendance at church wide worship services and Sticky Faith." [9]

Loving, Caring Adults Exude Belonging:

Even Just One Caring Adult Can Make an Impact
"Developmental research shows that having one or more caring adults in a child's life increases the likelihood that they will flourish, and become productive adults themselves. Children and adolescents who have a formal or informal "mentor-like" relationship with someone outside their home are less likely to have externalizing behavior problems (bullying) and internalizing problems (depression)." [10]

Non-Parental Adults Can Make an Impact
"Research has demonstrated that significant non-parental adults play a very important role in the lives of children and adolescents. This has been shown both through studies that utilize youth self-report (Blyth, Hill, & Thiel, 1982; Galbo & Demetrulias, 2001; Hendry, Roberts, Glendinning, & Coleman, 1992; Munsch & Blyth, 1993) and by more rigorous outcome studies (Werner, 1992, 1995; Zimmerman & Bingenheimer, 2002)." [11]

Trusting Relationships Can Help High-Risk Kids
"Further evidence of the protective impact of relationships with non-parental adults is found in the results from a 32 year longitudinal resiliency study of

children born in Kauai in the year 1955, conducted by Werner and colleagues. This study identified the existence of supportive, non-parental adults who developed trusting relationships with youth as one of five clusters of protective factors that were present in the lives of high-risk children who successfully adapted to adult life. These non-parental adults included grandparents, elder mentors, teachers, youth leaders and members of church groups (Werner, 1992, 1995)." [12]

Believe Research

So we've shown the importance of belonging through research and now we are going to take a look at believing.

Imagine going into a major surgery at your local hospital only to find out that your surgeon had not read or studied any of her textbooks in medical school. "Stop! Do not wheel me into the back room!" you'd exclaim. As her patient you would assume that she was mentored by more experienced surgeons (highly relational), that she participated in her practicum (truly experiential), and that she had a working knowledge of her field of practice (truly Scriptural or in this case, truly medical). Just as you would want your surgeon to have a working knowledge of human anatomy, how much more we want the kids in our ministry to have the knowledge, message and wisdom of the Bible that leads them to salvation in the gospel of Jesus Christ. This is the power of believe.

The need for "biblical literacy" among children may not be the most highly attended workshop at a conference, yet it is one of our most foundational and significant needs for the church in North America. Since 2014, our leadership team has conducted over 1,000 conversations with those who work with children and students in the local church. One of the emerging themes has been a disappointment—we would even say a lamenting—that their children and youth ministry has adopted a "Bible-lite" strategy that is characterized by morality-based teaching or virtues-based teaching. This strategy is a major contributor to what Christian Smith has termed "moralistic therapeutic deism" and has been quite harmful to the long-term vitality of the church and in the lives of disciples in much the same way as the metaphorical surgeon above who does not know her "source" information through her textbooks.

RESEARCH SHOWS THAT KIDS WHO HAVE A HIGHER ENGAGEMENT IN THE BIBLE ARE FAR MORE LIKELY TO LOVE AND FOLLOW JESUS INTO ADULTHOOD.

The Bible is our "source" information and research shows that kids who have a higher engagement in the Bible are far more likely to love and follow Jesus into adulthood. Even as some churches have gravitated to a Bible-lite strategy, many are not going that direction. Churches that elevate a highly scriptural model of discipleship tend to teach the gospel story as the thread of redemption from Genesis to Revelation, teach the Bible as a central part of their ministry, present the gospel to kids and students, value Scripture memory as a methodology and create a system to encourage Bible engagement as a consistent spiritual discipline.

Here's some research pertaining to believing:

Higher Spiritual Health
LifeWay Research wanted to know the "best predictors of spiritual health among young adults" and the number one finding was that the "child regularly read the Bible while growing up" [13]

Childhood Bible Reading
"Twenty-nine percent of the young adults regularly read the Bible while growing up, according to their parents. On average, that group has 12.5% higher spiritual health than otherwise comparable individuals who didn't, LifeWay Research found." [14]

Children Are Open to the Gospel
The Barna group has found that, "nearly half of all Americans who accept Jesus Christ as their Savior do so before reaching the age of 13 (43%), and that two out of three born again Christians (64%) made that commitment to Christ before their 18th birthday." [15]

Bible Engagement Benefit

In David Kinnaman and Mark Matlock's Faith for Exiles, *they found that 87% of those defined as "resilient disciples" feel closer to God when they read the Bible (compared to 44% habitual churchgoers, 21% unchurched, and 10% prodigals).* [16]

The Bible's Power to Transform

"Overall, almost six in 10 U.S. adults (58%) believe that the message of the Bible has transformed their life, including three in 10 (28%) who agree strongly with this statement ... Married adults and those with children under 18 are both more likely to indicate that the Bible has been life-changing" [17]

We were curious about what children's ministry leaders thought, so we have conducted four research projects (from 2013 - 2019) to discover what those in children's ministry find to be most important. When respondents were asked to rate the importance of 16 components, they rated Bible teaching as the most highly rated component as a 4.9 on a 5 point scale. This indicates nearly every respondent rated Bible teaching as a 5 (very important)! [18] In our 2014 research project, we wanted to understand what success looked like for children's ministry activities. So respondents were asked to rate 10 distinct potential ministry purposes–they were asked, "How important do you think each of these ministry purposes is?" Once again, they value the Bible above and beyond every other purpose for childrens' ministry. The statement "Helping children develop a love for studying and knowing the Bible" was the most highly-rated purpose (4.8 average on a 5 point scale), 98.3% rated this purpose as important or very important. [19]

In Matthew 28, Jesus commands His followers to go and **make disciples**. This is our calling and our commission: to teach kids the commandments and the ways of Jesus and to help them know how to call on the name of the Lord and be saved. Churches that are highly Scriptural are far better stewards of helping children and students believe.

Become Research

Now let's take a look at the research on the third component of resilient child discipleship on becoming.

A few years ago I (Matt) was sensing the need for adventure so I decided to lead a 5th grade boys small group. What could be more adventurous than that?! I could sense there was a restlessness with these emerging young men. Something was just not quite right. I began to sense that these guys were ready to explore new conversations. After some think–time and prayer, I asked our kids pastor for special permission to set aside the curriculum for a while and chart some new territory. My express intent was to help these guys navigate the world they were emerging into as 11-year-old boys. The months that followed delivered on pure adventure! We focused on their questions, key topics to navigate life and culture, the Bible and lots and lots of conversation. The nagging feeling God placed in my spirit was right. They certainly needed relationship. They absolutely needed Bible teaching. But they also needed more—they needed navigational help—they needed someone to walk beside them and help them become.

Parents, church leaders and child disciple makers, we must practice navigating real life conversations with kids and students. Whether it's science, the Bible, the sexual revolution, gender identity, the cultural divide, whatever—navigation simply means we will walk alongside, guide them, be co-learners with them and faithfully point them to Christ and His Word. Children and students do not expect us to be experts who have all of the answers, but they do expect us to engage. Engaging means asking questions. Engaging means we sometimes respond by saying, "I don't know, but maybe we should explore that together." Engaging means having compassion and empathy. And engaging also means we share the knowledge and wisdom we do have or even searching the Scriptures and praying together. The important part is this continual collision of belong (relationship), believe (the Bible, faith in Jesus) and become (help them navigate and experience life with them). Although conversation is foundational, it's just one way we express becoming (truly experiential).

Here's some research pertaining to becoming:

Conversation Is Critical
In Kara Powell and Chap Clark's Sticky Faith *research, they asked graduating high school seniors what they wished they had more of in youth group. Of the thirteen options we provided, their number one answer was "time for deep conversation." [20]*

We Need to Be Prepared for the Hard Conversations
Unfortunately, many adults are fearful of this type of experience with children and youth. In the Barna Group's research on Gen Z, they say, "It's important for pastors, leaders and parents to be prepared to discuss the real issues of the Christian faith, historical evidence, origins of the Bible, science, and inter-faith dialogue. This is the "acid-test" for real belief in the next generation. [21]

We Need to Engage, Not Avoid
A Barna group study in 2018 showed that only 68% of protestant youth pastors were comfortable talking about the origins of the Bible and historical evidence. Only 48% felt comfortable talking about science and the Bible and only 44% felt they could talk about inter-faith dialogues. The majority of teens (over 59% in all categories) felt uncomfortable talking about these things." [22]

Students Who Mentor Children Remain in the Faith
Students who serve and build relationships with younger children also tend to have stickier faith. [23]

Serving Cultivates Caring and Faith
Faith becomes more long-term when we take the time to find out what causes our kids are concerned about and we help them invest in those causes. We can cultivate caring, compassion and living on-mission when we serve together as a small group or as families. [24]

> *CHILDREN AND STUDENTS DO NOT EXPECT US TO BE EXPERTS WHO HAVE ALL THE ANSWERS, BUT THEY DO EXPECT US TO ENGAGE.*

Chris Marchand has been known to say, "We have to get kids outside of the simulation of the local church." Meaning, **faith is forged in the real experiences of life.** Faith can be cemented when we are doing real, practical hands-on engagement. When we give children and youth "truly experiencial" ministry, we are more likely to help them become like Jesus.

Resilient disciples do not simply engage in a simulation (learning about faith), but they bump up against the culture and they engage the world around them on mission for Chist. This very idea of getting kids active and engaged can be influenced and cultivated from a young age.

Christian Smith's words at the beginning of this section tend to echo in our hearts and minds when he says, "... no single factor can produce high levels of emerging adult religiousness. Instead, multiple combinations of factors working together are necessary to more likely than not produce that outcome." Time and time again, the factors that are known to produce long-term fruit in the lives of children and youth are the three critical components of Resilient Child Discipleship.

What keeps you up at night?

One of the most challenging conversations we hear from local church leaders is the fast pace and the sheer volume of tasks and projects you lead and steward in local church ministry. We hurt for you. You have a big job, and there is no more important mission than the church. As you captivate our mind space, we wonder about your sleepless nights ... what must keep you up as you bravely face unprecedented cultural upheaval? We share these sleepless nights with you. One of the things that keeps us up at night is our worry for all that you carry. Our prayer for you in this season is that you are able to find the space to have the critical conversation that NASA must have had. If propulsion, navigation and human life support are what has to be solved to achieve our mission, what must be stopped, paused or changed? What will it take to place increased focus on the essentials ... the few, key contributing factors that are known to influence mission impact?

We can only imagine the challenges you must weigh as you think about how to design and implement a child discipleship system (team, program, methods, communication, volunteers, etc.) that's an integration of highly relational ministry (Belong), deeply scriptural ministry (Believe) and truly experiential ministry (Become). These are the few, key contributing factors that lead to long-term discipleship.

Belong, Believe **and** ***Become*** **are the foundation for spiritual resilience. And the Church of 2050 will require just that.**

In the next chapter, we will discuss the essential challenges we must face as we implement effective child discipleship and shape the fearless future of the church. Let's stick together!

ESSENTIAL QUESTIONS:

As you think about your children's ministry, what are you doing that's having the most positive impact on making disciples? Can you measure, track or evaluate this impact? If so, how?

Within your children's ministry, what are you doing that's having the least impact? Have you considered pausing or stopping this particular methodology or activity? Would it be possible to repurpose this energy, capacity or resource more effectively?

As you think about the challenge within the NASA metaphor, what else could your team pause or stop in order to focus on fewer factors with higher impact?

Do you see "belong, believe, become" reflected in your story or others around you? What would it look like to build your children's ministry around belonging, believing and becoming with the aim of maximizing lifelong impact, cultural engagement and the church of 2050?

A 2050
RESILIENT
STRATEGY

CHAPTER 11

We continue to be led by a vision for the 2050 church. But is it even possible to predict the kind of leadership the future church will need, the kind of leadership we should be building into today's kids?

One of Scripture's most insightful descriptions of leadership gives us an answer to those questions. Here is the setting:

King Saul has banished David from Israel. At this point in their story, Saul still wears the crown, but David has won the people's hearts. A defection of mighty men who had served under Saul has begun. *"Day after day men came to help David at Hebron, until he had a great army, like the army of God. They were brave warriors, ready for battle and able to handle the shield and spear. Their faces were the faces of lions, and they were swift as gazelles in the mountains." (1 Chronicles 12:8, 32, NIV)*

Scripture lists the new followers by tribal names and by the size of the tribe. From Judah, carrying shield and spear—6,800 armed for battle. That is how they are listed in the biblical account. But one tribe is the exception. One tribe stands out from the rest.

> *"From Issachar, men who understood the times, and knew what Israel should do—200 chiefs, with all their relatives in command."*
> *(1 Chronicles 12:32, NIV)*

These men from Issachar were Old Testament culture vultures. Maybe they could sense where David might be threatened, where an enemy might attack or what force was gathering on the horizon. But they did more than sense, analyze, warn and project. Scripture says they knew what to do. What might that have looked like? Well maybe they knew what needed to be done to defend David's safety and the future kingdom, or what David's army strategy should be, or who should lead and who should follow. They probably could read how attitudes were changing, how David was winning Israel's heart, but **then they knew what to do about it ...** how to direct the peoples' shifting loyalties towards actually making young David their king.

That's called strategy and it is a remarkable aspect of leadership. We are in desperate need of that kind of leadership today. It seems there are many expert analysts. A lot of people can say, "This is where things are messed up today." They can read the times and provide appropriate data, charts and graphs. While that's a good thing, it's not enough. It takes a special kind of leadership gift to move beyond analysis to solutions—actually knowing what to do.

We have dedicated a lot of time and space in this book to describing the times we are living in, and the trends and the challenges facing this generation. We have analyzed the effects of screen discipleship, family breakdown, church decline and public opposition some of the mountains kids are facing today.

But we have done more. We have looked beyond today to 2050, and wondered if we are preparing our kids for a future time of potential challenge for the church. We have examined how public acceptance of Christian views is deteriorating to the point that by 2050, if not sooner, our views, our public moral conscience, our Christian voice may be denounced, or worse, sought to be silenced. The landscape of 2050 with its resistance to Christianity is a huge mountain range the future church will need to scale and conquer.

That is analysis. But where is strategy?

What if we brought together the collective wisdom of today's Issachar-type leaders? What if we could develop a Resilient Child Discipleship strategy that "understood the times and knew what to do?"

That would create a movement! A fire would be lit from the children's' wing of the church that would ignite a movement of God's Spirit and strengthen the church for generations to come.

In the previous chapter we asked, What if the KidMin community decided to unite together as essentialists? What if we decided as a community to focus in on the simple factors that contribute to long-term discipleship in the lives of kids? Could we cut through the clutter and abandon the tasks that steal our time, yet yield low results? WOW—imagine the collective impact!

Those are the kinds of questions asked by Issachar-type leaders. So in that spirit of leadership we would like to put forward a strategy, a plan for moving into 2015 to build a discipleship foundation for this generation of children.

1 *PRAYER OF A DIFFERENT KIND*

Where should we begin in formulating a 2050 resilient strategy? We should begin with prayer. Today's church needs to be committed to prayer in ways we have never prayed before.

Consider that we actually need to pray differently than we have for any other modern generation of kids. We need to pray that the generations of "screen disciples" growing up today will have a collision with their Creator, and understand that they belong to Him, above all else. We need to pray that they will be resilient disciples—people who love Jesus for the rest of their lives.

Our prayers need to claim this generation and the ones that follow for Christ. We need to pray that their identities will be in Jesus, their belonging found within the church. We must pray and ask God to give our children the courage to stand in the middle of a perverse and crooked generation as lights and proclaim, "I am not that. I am this. The church is my group. These people are my people. This is my choice ... to love Jesus for the rest of my life."

Ajith Fernando presented a message for a Lausanne conference that described how Jesus prayed for his own disciples. [1] I found it extremely insightful. In His message called *Developing Disciples Jesus' Way*, he referenced John 17:11. Jesus is praying to God for His disciples. *Holy Father, keep them in Your name, which You have given me, that they may be one, even as We are one.* In other words, Keep them safe. Keep them protected from influences they are not ready for. Keep them in Your name.

IT TAKES A SPECIAL KIND OF LEADERSHIP GIFT TO MOVE BEYOND ANALYSIS TO SOLUTIONS— ACTUALLY KNOWING WHAT TO DO.

Keep them identified with You. Safe in Your care.

But, Jesus doesn't stop there. With a nod to the incubation period and the tender early spiritual years, He then prays a very different prayer over his disciples. *"I have given them Your word; and the world has hated them because they are not of the world, just as I am not of the world. I do not ask that You take them out of the world, but that You keep them from the evil one."* (John 17:14-21) ... that the world may believe that You have sent me.

THEN WE NEED TO BRAVELY PRAY THEM OUT INTO THE WORLD, TO ENGAGE IT DESPITE ITS HOSTILITY.

Clearly Jesus understood the risks facing his disciples after His death when they engaged the world. But it was also critically important that the disciples grow past their incubation period of safety to engage the world so that the world could believe.

Following Jesus' way of praying for his disciples we should pray that this generation would stay "in his name" identified with Christ and the gospel for the rest of their lives. This includes protection from the evil one. But we can't yield to temptation to stop there. Then we need to bravely pray them out into the world, to engage it despite its hostility. In other words, to be witnesses.

We can purpose and strategize to raise our Christian kids "in the world" and also "kept in His name" but with the purpose of them growing up to be influencers—Christian writers, Christian best-selling authors, Christian journalists, Christian movie producers, Christian politicians, Christian college professors, Christian bloggers and podcasters. This should be part of a strategy to push back against being silenced as the moral conscience in an increasingy dark world.

2 *ALLEGIANCE AND IDENTITY*

A second goal of a 2050 resilient strategy: allegiance and identity. Church attendance matters. Children and youth ministry leaders need to own the allegiance and identity message and make it clear.

The symptomatic problem of sporadic church attendance among "church going" families today points to allegiances that are to lesser things. When our identities are in Christ, church attendance will follow. "Being there" is such an important part of belonging and building resilient discipleship into our kids, we shouldn't deceive ourselves into thinking it really doesn't matter. Kids who drop out, the 50% we are watching leave the church today, we suspect are kids whose "belonging" was a weak and sporadic attachment. As young kids, they went with the program. Or not. But when they matured into young adulthood, then we could see how weak their attachment to the body of Christ actually was all along. Low attendance is potentially a warning symptom of things to come.

Someone needs to take up this banner and wave it. Wait! That someone is us! KidMin messaging needs to embrace "Be here!" and "You belong here!" as a united theme. Being present is such an important part of belonging that we need to make sure our families hear this loud and clear from the KidMin community. We own that message. Let's say it as one voice. For the sake of the 2050 church, today's kids need to have church time prioritized. The velocity of secular culture bombarding our kids today needs to be met with an insistence on church attendance—the basics for membership in anything else.

LOW ATTENDANCE IS POTENTIALLY A WARNING SYMPTOM OF THINGS TO COME.

3 *RESILIENCE*

**Then a third goal in a 2050 resilient strategy—resilience.
We need to be sure that the DNA of KidMin is built on belong,
believe, become discipleship with the goal of resilience.**

Go ahead and bring on the fun, the games, the craziness and the joy that belongs to ministry to kids. We love it too! But all that programming must also support three essentials ... belong, believe and become. These three words capture the profound pattern and direction of a child's spiritual development into resilient discipleship. Is this how we are intentionally reaching kids in our KidMin programs?

Belonging, believing and becoming looks like the story of David Dickenson. One day, when David was 8-years-old, his father went to work and never came home. The police discovered he had cashed a paycheck after work and then vanished into oblivion. The police believed he had been followed to the place where he cashed his check, was then robbed, killed and his body dumped into Lake Michigan.

Without income and a massive amount of hardships, David and his family struggled significantly for many years. Even as a little boy, David helped support his family with paper routes and odd jobs, but there was barely enough money for them to survive.

One of David's most crushing moments occurred when a teacher looked him in the eyes and said, "David you're stupid and will never amount to anything." The teacher's words were like a magic spell over David's life. For years, they held a power of negative belief that David ran with. Words have the power to write and rewrite the narratives that children believe, and David carried those words for a very long time.

But there was a church! This is where David's life took a dramatic turn. A church man, a leader in Awana, understood what belonging was all about. Even though David was clearly a troubled child, it didn't scare this loving, caring adult from building a relationship with him and making a huge impact on his life. One of these moments came when a father-son event at their church was announced. Realizing that a deep void of a missing father was pulling on young David's heart, this man leaned over and said, "David, I only have girls. Would you go to the father-son event with me?" You can imagine how that made David feel. Here's someone who owed him nothing but had given him such richness. This loving, caring adult was there for David every week. He helped him memorize Scripture, and David begin to believe that he wasn't stupid like the teacher had said. In fact, he was one of the best Bible memorizers in his club! David received grace in these moments. No longer did he need to cart around the shame, but rather, with each relational touch point with this loving, caring adult, the grace of God was reprogramming David's heart. David moved from a place of loneliness to belonging and through the attention of a loving, caring adult into believing.

David's story has another dark twist. It concerned the truth about his father. Decades after his disappearance, they discovered that David's father had not died. In some ways, the truth was worse than death. He had abandoned his family on his way home from work that day. He moved far away, remarried and had a new family of his own. His new children were named with the same names of David and his siblings.

As heartbreaking as that story is, David is a resilient disciple today. He pastors a church that has an extensive discipleship ministry to children and David is in the thick of it—driving kids back and forth in the church bus and actively involved in every aspect of club every week. David knows the power of relationships in the lives of children. He understands the importance of the gospel and the belong, believe, become pathway, and how God's Word can rewrite the narratives in the lives of children today.

WHAT IF WHEN WE OPENED OUR MOUTHS THE LOVE OF GOD CAME RUSHING FORTH?

4 *INSPIRE VOLUNTEERS TO BECOME LEADERS*

Then a fourth goal of a 2050 resilient strategy is leadership. We need to stop just volunteering and start leading.

David's story is an outstanding example of a loving, caring adult whose relationship went far beyond the definition of "volunteer." We need to take a serious look at that word "volunteer" and some of the things it implies. Volunteering keeps the door open for other possibilities. "Maybe I'll be there to work in KidMin—or not. I am, after all, just a volunteer." When churches struggle to get volunteers we think that's not what children need today anyway. Honestly, this generation of kids need specialists, generational guardians and faithful dedicated leaders.

Awana is a 70-plus-year-old ministry. One of the most amazing parts of the Awana story is the large number of leaders who have been working with kids for decades. I always ask them "Why?" Why did you show up every week? Why did you say, "No" to other things you would have enjoyed doing? What got into you?

Their answers are amazingly similar; "I just fell in love with the kids."

Whether they kept attendance roles, provided snacks or taught kids the Bible, we think of them as more than volunteers. They are leaders. They led with their priorities. They led with their time. They led with their presence. They led with their hearts.

KidMin needs more leaders and fewer volunteers! Ministry to children is the most critical ministry in the church impacting the future of faith. It should be funded, prioritized, preached about from the pulpit, and celebrated constantly. It needs our investment, our time and our lives. In light of the challenges facing this generation of kids, they deserve the most charismatic, energized, enthusiastic leaders we can find. Our churches need to understand how critical this is.

It's time to do what leaders do. It's time to lead.

5 *REDEMPTION OF TECHNOLOGY*

Then a final piece of a 2050 resilient strategy is the redemption of technology.

Technology is powerful and it is not going away. Yes, we need to place boundaries around it limiting access to influences, and to our time. But we can do more. We need to invest in finding ways to maximize its discipleship potential in kids' lives.

```
We are asking questions like:


How could we link a global community of Christian kids for
prayer, fellowship and connection?

How can we facilitate resilient discipleship in the palm of
kids' hands today?

How can we have a greater presence, impact and future through
the use of technology?

How can a loving, caring adult model to a child that authentic
relationship is best experienced in a real person-to-person
relationship?

How can a disciple maker help a child see that technology is
there to facilitate authentic relationship and not the other
way around?
```

Maybe you are asking these question and more. In Awana's corner of KidMin we are introducing a new digital Sunday curriculum called ***brite*** * that focuses on resilient discipleship. We know this is necessary and we are excited about launching into the digital, learning

WE ARE STANDING ON THE EDGE OF A TECHNOLOGICAL AGE THAT COULD BE AS TRANSFORMATIVE AND IMPACTING, AS INCLUSIVE AND GOSPEL SPREADING AS ANY THE CHURCH HAS PREVIOUSLY EXPERIENCED.

world. But this is just the beginning of the possibilities for exciting new ways of spreading the gospel into a digitally linked world. In 2050, discipleship will be learned in ways we couldn't imagine today. An amazing 2050 world, unknown to us today, stretches out before us and calls us to its way of discipling. Not only is 2050 a challenge to believing, it is also an opportunity to reach our world with a capacity we have never before experienced.

Bring on the gospel-informed creative world-impacting ideas!

Bring on the Christ-following technology developers!

Bring on the missional-living financiers and dream facilitators!

We are standing on the edge of a technological age that could be as transformative and impacting, as inclusive and gospel-spreading as any age the church has previously experienced. If Luther and Tyndale changed their worlds by translating the Bible into "every man's" language, the technological age could change the world by putting the gospel and discipleship into "every man's" hand.

Our 2050 vision has discipleship potential like we have never before seen. Captivating. We should all get together to think, dream and pray about this.

ESSENTIAL QUESTIONS:

Do we belong to Jesus? Or are our interests, allegiances and passions pointing somewhere else?

Is the KidMin community deeply, passionately in love with Jesus? Does it show?

Are we resilient disciples?

Do you and your leaders belong to Jesus? Have you heard their testimonies and salvation stories? If so, spend some time remembering with them. If not, jumpstart the question and probe deeper.

Who's that one kid that God has placed in your path that you need to take the first step with? What is going on in their basement that needs the story that God has placed in your life?

Is the gospel personally, clearly and regularly presented to every child in your ministry? Can every leader explain salvation and why it matters?

What 2050 strategy could you implement in your ministry to make resilient disciples?

DEAR DISCIPLE MAKER,

Years ago, when you said "Yes" to working with kids at church a couple of hours a week did you think:

a   *Rats! Why can't I say no to that KidMin pastor?*

b   *OK, well, I'm not crazy about this, but I can do anything for a year.*

c   *I'm really not great with kids, maybe I can direct parking or take attendance.*

When did everything change? When did you start to actually care? How did that mid-week program for kids become the highlight of your week? And that bossy little girl who talks too much and could run a small developing country, when did she wheedle her way into your heart? And that little boy who asked everyone to pray for his father because "he doesn't know Jesus", when did he become a son you care for so deeply?

Every week you project your voice and stand tall, you instruct, you drill, you train, all the while trying to corral a roomful of kid energy. But still, they run circles around you. They ignore your instructions until you start counting down. They are boisterous and physical with each other and someone nearly always ends up upset or in tears. Every week it's a lot of kid drama. But strangely, every night you come home feeling energized, full of life and in love with every kid there.

And more, you feel the smile of God over your life. It's the best two hours of your week by far and, deep inside, you know it's the most important thing you could be doing with your life.

Think of all the years you've said "Yes!" to kids. You've led many boys and girls to accept Jesus as their Savior. You've helped them to hide God's Word in their hearts where it has formed a foundation for a lifetime of discipleship. You have done your job so well.

But here's something you may not realize. You may be the single most important factor in some children's lives. You are the caring adult providing constancy, stability and safety. You are two hours of love every week that felt like home and belonging and all-is-wellness.

You are more important than you know.

These children are growing up and soon will forget your name. But when they think of God's love . . . to them it looks a lot like you. God laughing at their jokes, high fiving them, greeting them with heart-felt welcome, loving them to Jesus and a belonging no worldly pleasure can provide.

A CHURCH AT THE CROSSROADS OF CULTURAL CHANGE

CHAPTER 12

If you've made it to this point, then we know you're all in on creating resilient disciples.

Together, we've come quite a ways. We've defined our cultural and church realities, providing a pathway forward. We've examined the declining influence of the church and we have presented a ministry philosophy that we are truly convinced will help shape children to love Jesus for a lifetime.

Now we find ourselves here, at the end of our conversation together. Our eyes are on the future, our hearts are with the 2050 church. From all we've examined, it looks like the 2050 church could be a church in the margins, a church that is less a part of mainstream thought and less tolerated.

Let's project what life lived in the margins might be like. Let's look at a point of history, back to a people who fully loved Jesus and followed Him from the margins of society and culture. Let's look at the church found in the book of Acts.

As Luke begins his letter, we call the Acts of the Apostles (Acts), his aim is to provide an account of how the disciples and others who followed Jesus (those who belonged to, believed in and strove to become like Jesus) found themselves in a post-resurrection and post-ascension reality. It must have been hard to follow Jesus throughout His earthly life. It was certainly hard to follow Him leading up to His death, so much so that those who gave up everything to follow Him scattered and fled. Even Peter, the Rock, denied Jesus at the questioning of a little girl, but at least when Jesus was alive on earth he could be seen, heard, touched and talked to in a very visible way. How would it now be without Him, Jesus, their rabbi, and friend, present?

OUR EYES ARE ON THE FUTURE, OUR HEARTS ARE WITH THE 2050 CHURCH.

As the Book of Acts begins, we see a people whose convictions have led them to the margins of culture. Acts 2 opens with the following famous church passage:

> When the day of Pentecost arrived, they were all together in one place. (Acts 2:1)

When we church people read Acts 2:1 we immediately say, "This is us!" Indeed, this is a snapshot of the earliest church; a people of diverse backgrounds, but a singular belief in Jesus, belonging to Him and to one another. This is a crowd of 120 assembled together during a cultural holiday, gathered together in one place. And for a lot of us who love Jesus and His church, this is where we stop. Why can't it just be "just us?" Saved, singled out, separated from society, but safe. It reminds me of Peter, James and John at the transfiguration when Peter suggests that they just stay up there with Jesus, Moses and Elijah. Isn't that what we see here? These men and women were set apart due to their faith and don't we see them here, together? Isn't that all we need?

Keep reading ...

Acts 2:1 is a setup. It is the starting point, not the finish line. God, through the Holy Spirit, empowered this group of highly unlikely Jesus followers to start more than the first Christian club. This was the start of an expansive, thriving, far-reaching body of believers who boldly built the kingdom of God and continued the work of Jesus. This was the birth of the church; proclaiming and practicing all that Jesus commanded to those both near and far.

This group of scared men and women (who were increasingly different from their culture due to their convictions) didn't cloister themselves into a holy huddle, remembering the "good old days" with Jesus and eventually fading away. They were used by God, empowered by the Holy Spirit, at the crossroads of cultural change. Acts shows us a church that does anything but conforms, stays silent and slowly dies. For those who love Jesus and His church, Acts is both the canvas and the color of our picture of the church.

The church: It is a people whose love for Jesus leads them to love others. It is a people who speak the many languages of the culture around them (in the case of Acts 2:4, this was a literal event). It is a people who are moved with compassion and stand with courage and conviction. It is a demonstration of what happens when lives change through the power of the Holy Spirit. Acts 2:4 is a wonderful image of the birth of the church as we know it. Spine and heart, loving Jesus and loving others, filled with grace and truth, this is the church of Acts. Bold, beautiful, abounding in generosity, teaching, empowering, praying, worshiping, sharing, eating together (Amen!) and thriving from the margins! It is a community diverse in makeup, but unified in mission. It is a worshipping body of believers willing to sacrifice everything for the one thing that matters. It is unlikely relationships resulting in unrelenting faith. It is a movement that spreads from person to person, community to community, region to region. It is the Great Commission being lived out in real-time.

Our vision for the 2050 church, the church at the crossroads of cultural change, is not some pie-in-the-sky imaginary vision without basis. The church has been here before. A biblically-based reality of a church struggling to live engaged a culture that marginalizes it is found throughout the New Testament. We are the continuation of building that very church, birthed in the book of Acts. We just happen to be deeply convicted about the fact that resilient discipleship (which renews the church to this vision) starts in the hearts and lives of children and youth.

This small group of believers began to grow, rapidly. The gospel is like that, it spreads. As a former pastor and church planter, I (Mike) cannot read Acts 2 without reading all the way to the end …

> *And they devoted themselves to the apostles' teaching and the fellowship, to the breaking of bread and the prayers. And awe came upon every soul, and many wonders and signs were being done through the apostles. And all who believed were together and had all things in common. And they were selling their possessions and belongings and distributing the proceeds to all, as any had need. And day by day, attending the temple together and breaking bread in their homes, they received their food with glad and generous hearts, praising God and having favor with all the people. And the Lord added to their number day by day those who were being saved. (Acts 2:42-47)*

This is a beautiful picture of a vibrant, living, growing church. The culture did not change. This body of believers was still marginalized, living under constant scrutiny and persecution. Its leaders were arrested, even killed for living their lives as followers of Jesus. Yet even in the midst of such opposition, the church grew both inwardly (in love for Jesus and one another) and outwardly (as more and more were being saved). And out of this, a movement was birthed that would sweep the world. Persecution only added passion and passion fueled obedience and obedience led to exponential growth of the gospel throughout regions near and far.

However, this resilience was more than hard work and Holy Spirit hustle—though both certainly helped. The church flourished with the help of men and women who supported the work through any means necessary. In Acts we meet men like Barnabas and women like Lydia, individuals who invested in the early church and the works of the apostles in order to provide means through which the gospel might spread. As we leaf through the New Testament, we can see others who do the same. John Rinehart, in his book *Gospel Patrons,* says they are people who "acted to meet the extraordinary need with extraordinary generosity." Barnabas, Lydia, Pricilla, Aquila and Phoebe are all mentioned in Acts and Paul's Epistles as men and women who used their means to support the ministry of the gospel. Even Jesus, the perfect Son of God had help sustaining His ministry.

In Luke's account of Jesus' life we read:

> *Soon afterward He [Jesus] went on through cities and villages, proclaiming and bringing the good news of the kingdom of God. And the twelve were with Him, and also some women who had been*

PERSECUTION ONLY ADDED PASSION AND PASSION FUELED OBEDIENCE AND OBEDIENCE LED TO EXPONENTIAL GROWTH OF THE GOSPEL

healed of evil spirits and infirmities: Mary, called Magdalene, from whom seven demons had gone out, and Joanna, the wife of Chuza, Herod's household manager, and Susanna, and many others, who provided for them out of their means. (Luke 8:1-3)

Gospel patrons (Rinehart's phrase) have been offering sustainability for the work of the gospel to scale from the time Jesus was doing ministry. The sacred work of salvation need not suffer from scarcity! Gospel patronage would continue to accompany the growth of the church through centuries of persecution and in very oppressive places.

If you're reading this book (and the Bible) in English, you are reaping the benefits of gospel patronage. In 1523 a young preacher named William Tyndale met a wealthy merchant named Humphrey Monmouth. At that point in history the Bible's standard translation was in Latin. This was deemed the only holy and allowed version of God's Word, it was backed and enforced by the authorities and powers of the time, after all it had been trusted and untouched for over a thousand years. Yet the Latin Vulgate (the name of the Bible of the time) was largely inaccessible to the masses.

While Luther was translating the Scriptures in Germany, Tyndale was desperate to do the same for people living throughout England, yet he couldn't do it alone. He was passionate to see the Bible made available for anyone throughout the British Empire and was responsible for translating the New Testament into English; mass-producing it on the newest technology, the printing press. Tyndale did the work. Monmouth made it possible.

Monmouth funded the work of Tyndale, and at great cost. Both men were arrested and their public reputations were destroyed. Monmouth's home was raided, his fortunes dwindled down. He spent a year in the Tower of London, without heat, without comfort. Tyndale would be betrayed, arrested and executed.

THE CHILDREN IN OUR CHURCHES TODAY ARE THE LEADERS OF THE CHURCH OF 2050

What does a 16th Century Bible translator or his benefactor have to do with you or me in the 21st Century? Like Monmouth we have the ability to fuel significant movements of God. The children in our churches today are the leaders of the church of 2050. Our investment in God's work in their lives could produce world-changing results. After all, you're probably not reading the Vulgate today, but your English Bible. What if Tyndale didn't have the backing of Monmouth? What if Barnabas didn't sell his property and give it to the early church? What if this movement, this call to focus on resilient discipleship didn't have you?

Without you, this movement becomes just another book on the bookshelf. That's all.

Allow me to be clear, your gospel patronage may actually be financially funding the work of the gospel in your church or throughout the world. Or, it may be the time you invest in the lives God has entrusted to you in your church and community. We may not be certain of the future outcomes of our time, resource or financial investments in the kingdom; but we can have absolute certainty regarding our present opportunities. Your investment might be the constant catalyst needed to set the spark of the next "Great Gospel Awakening." We firmly believe that this revival fire will begin in the hearts of children, perhaps the children in your own church!

So let's look at one of the most vibrant and exciting examples of a church living out what we've been dreaming about.

This is a church alive and vibrant in her community. In the midst of cultural change, she has not altered her views or compromised her stand, nor has she sheltered herself away; instead, she has opened her arms wider to be a place of refuge, grace and truth. While a fence may surround her property line, there is no gate that closes out the neighborhood. Her parking lot is full of chalk drawings, hopscotch games and scribbled mermaids. There are spaces for expectant mothers, families with children who have special needs, seniors as well as those with disabilities because all generations and abilities belong here.

If you were to arrive at a weekend service, you would be greeted as soon as you pull in by an elderly couple and their granddaughter smiling and waving, extending warmth to you and the other cars entering the lot. As you park and exit your car, you'd see kids playing on the property, hear the laughter of tag and hide and seek. You'd see toddlers wobbling and waddling on the soft grass by the flower beds while moms and aunties exchange the latest stories with laughter.

Upon entering the lobby, your eyes cannot help taking in the beautiful art and media. The walls are a gallery expressing the worship of God through both curated reproductions of famous works as well as many within the congregation. However, not everything is professional, many of the pieces are done by children who may lack the refinement, but abound in joy and passion for the craft. This colorful place is only slightly more diverse than the people within the space. The lobby buzzes with conversation in multiple languages and dialects. Families and individuals living out their unique stories together is commonplace in this church. The potlucks and church dinners are a smorgasbord that would rival any international food festival with native dishes from India, Mexico, Honduras, the Carribean, Poland, Korea, Egypt, Pakistan, Thailand, Ethiopia, Albania, Ukraine and of course the standard American fare—after all, eating together is a sacred practice!

THIS IS A CHURCH ALIVE AND VIBRANT IN HER COMMUNITY.

As you make your way towards the sanctuary, you can't help but notice a space set up with pictures of people across a giant map. Some are local, some are on university and college campuses, some in neighboring states, cities and rural areas. Others are pictures in various places throughout the world. All have letters and notes addressed to the kids of this church telling the stories of the people whom this church has sent out to make disciples throughout the nations and seen God at work. All are thanking the people, and specifically, the children of this church for their dedication in prayer and generosity as well as their hearts to see those far from Jesus, no matter the setting, be brought near.

Like every other church there are announcements of news and upcoming events displayed. One is a thank you from the local public school district where members have been tutoring as well as coaching. Another tells of an upcoming young professionals gathering focused on the topic of generosity. One more that may catch your attention is that of the next "love thy neighborhood" gathering where the congregation adopts a subdivision or city block and showers it with service. These "good works" are gospel-centric missional movements of this local church.

Entering into the worship service, your ears are filled with the sounds of hearts being poured out before God in song. The congregation moves and sways as an ocean of praise within the sanctuary. Fathers are holding babies in one arm while raising the other arm in adoration. The voices of the most senior saints are harmoniously heard alongside the melodies springing up from the youngest of children. Hymns are offered up as an infant with special needs gets passed from family to family, she is loved in a way so undeniable and so selflessly. Grandparents are holding hands with their grandbabies and sons with their mothers. Men are alive and unashamed to sing, to cry out before God, to show that He alone is their strength. These are people who cannot worship their Lord enough and are filled with joy when they're able to do so together.

As you enter into the preaching of God's Word, the truth of Scripture is being unpacked with care and dedication. It is like a feast of daily bread being broken and offered to the hungry. It is undeniably rich, satisfying and wonderful. The light and life of biblical doctrine is offered to all with conviction and compassion, with love for God and for people. Each point fortifies the seeds of truth and is carried into the hearts and minds of the church family. Biblical doctrines and timeless truths are unpacked, explained and shared so that every level of listener, from the seasoned senior saint to the most distant spiritual seeker, understands the grace and truth offered from the text. It's transformational for all.

This small snapshot of a Sunday service is representative of this church. It is rooted in its community and stretches its arms out to the world. It cannot be defined by a single socio-economic status or class. It stewards its place in the community with passionate dedication; its members are involved and invested in committees, projects, clubs, boards and other places where gospel influence matters. Because of their community involvement, this church is able to bless more of those in need, to offer Godly counsel in times of tragedy and extend selfless service to those within their reach. This church is both highly relational and deeply committed.

So where can you find this vibrant, living, passionate place? How can you catch a service streaming online? When and where can you find this congregation coming together to worship?

You may be asking who's leading this community. Surely this pastor has written a book, has a blog or is developing content on some platform.

We want to welcome you to the resileint church of 2050 ... the church that has been loving Jesus for all of their lives.

> *THIS CHURCH IS BOTH HIGHLY RELATIONAL AND DEEPLY COMMITTED.*

ESSENTIAL QUESTIONS:

Does your team have a clearly defined vision and mission?

How are we still like the church described in Acts 2? How are we different?

What are ways you are living out "Gospel patronage" in your church or with other ministries you serve/support? Think in terms of time, resources, influence, investment.

Are you inviting others into opportunities to be the patrons of your ministry and be the ones fanning the flames of 2050 and beyond?

Take time to make an honest assessment of your thoughts, fears and feelings about 2050. What scares you that you can offer to Jesus in prayer? What excites you that you can also commit to Him? Ask Him to give you wisdom as we lead the children and youth in our churches.

Want to continue the conversation? Check out www. ***resilientdisciples.com*** *where you'll find articles, stories, podcasts, resources and a community of fire carriers like yourself who are all in for making resilient disciples!*

ACKNOWLEDGEMENTS

Can I tell you something that surprised me after I began working at Awana? I found there was more creativity and passion for mission, per square foot, at Awana than I have experienced almost anywhere else in the kingdom. I want to acknowledge some of that now.

A team of artists, wordsmiths, theologians and practitioners has dreamed about the message in this book for a long time. Matt Markins, our resident futurist, President and Chief Strategy Officer, has been amazingly creative about ways to spread the message of RESILIENT. He is more than a strategist or writer however. Through it all, Matt's leadership—strong in strategic details, writing and keeping our heads lifted—has been stellar. I feel so blessed to work with him.

Mike Handler, Chief Communications Officer, is one of the most creative people I know. I call him the extension of my right brain—whatever I dream up, he can make it better! He's quick-witted (with an uncanny ability to make us laugh) and a visual artist. He's also a beautiful soul who can pray like no one I've ever met. His writing has a spiritual depth and a love for God that's woven its way through RESILIENT wherever he touched it. He loves Awana and working with him is a joy.

Chris Marchand, Vice President of Partner Solutions is a force in the best way possible. In his role of overseeing the development of Awana curriculum, he is shepherding the spiritual development of a generation of Christian kids. A natural leader, communicator and passionate idealist, we can expect to hear more of his voice in the years ahead.

Additionally, a team of leaders at Awana has supported this book. A huge thank you goes out to Kevin White, Brian Rhodes, Chip Root, Cindy Craig, Ken Toller, Diego Mota, Michelle Albert, Kendra Stewart and Judy Reder. Also thank you to Debi Wall and my Executive Assistant, Deby Ammons. You. Are. The. Best.

On a personal note, I am indebted to my husband, Steve Bell, who is so much more than a husband where this book is concerned. He has listened to me and edited me. He has given his mind space to so many aspects of RESILIENT. There are no words to shine enough light on his contribution and life force. Thank you Steve, from the bottom of my heart.

Also, in a dark time of my life recently some people gave me the gift of presence. Jim and Cindy Judge did not let me walk through the darkness alone. Doug DeMerchant gave me amazing amounts of love, prayer and presence. Thank you. I love each of you dearly! Wess Stafford walked beside me with his extraordinary mercy gift, as did John R. Anderson. Brenda and Daryle Doden showed up in remarkable ways; and Shawn Thornton was my pastor of choice. My sons Brendan and Justin were more than sons to me. They were advisors, protectors and comforters. All of your care got me through the valley.

Finally, I owe a huge debt of gratitude to the Awana Board of Directors and Board Chairman, David Branton. Your selfless service and ability to lift your eyes from the history of Awana to the church's future, has made this journey possible. Thank you. I give you my highest compliment: you are resilient!

Valerie Bell
Chief Executive Officer

I'd like to first express thankfulness to my best friend and wife, Katie. I call you our family's "resident theologian" not only because of your vast knowledge of the Scriptures and many years of faithful study of the Bible, but because of your passion and pursuit of Jesus. You are my first source of wise counsel, strategic thinking and relational empathy. I can think of no better partner in ministry, and nothing is sweeter than your love and friendship.

I'd like to thank our thought leadership and writing team. Valerie, you gave us language for what we could not describe. You gave us vision to direct us out of chaos and pain. You are our leader, mentor and friend. Chris, you belong here. When you speak, heads turn. Your ability to think, plan, build, lead and manage is remarkable. Mike, my friend and my brother. You see farther down the path than most. And what you see is remarkable, it's beautiful and I want to be a part of it. I hope I can go far with you.

And lastly, I'd like to thank our team of leaders, collaborators, influencers and and builders: Kevin White, Brian Rhodes, Chip Root, Cindy Craig, Ken Toller, Diego Mota, Michelle Albert, Kendra Stewart, Deby Ammons, Debi Wall, Judy Reder, Mark Roman, Dan Lovaglia, Warren Markins, Hudson Markins and Melanie Hester. You. Are. Resilient. This collaborative process has been marked by love, gratitude and hospitality. These are the ways of Jesus and I love the culture this team is building.

Matt Markins
President, Chief Strategy Officer

I want to thank the following individuals; each one has had a significant impact on me and the content that I have contributed to this book.

I want to thank my wife, Tricia. Hand-in-hand and side-by-side, we have walked the road of ministry together. Thank you for being an incredible sounding board, an encouragement to me, and for your wisdom. I'm so glad that we get to do life together.

I want to thank both of my children. Being a parent has provided me with incredible experiences and moments that have shaped my discipleship in ways I couldn't imagine. Thanks for making time for "Dad conversations" at the dinner table, and for chasing down your curiosity as you seek out answers to your faith in Jesus Christ.

I want to thank all my colleagues at Awana Clubs International. Each of you has played a part in shaping and molding me and playing an active role in my discipleship. I'm forever thankful for your strength, humility, wisdom, and courage.

Chris Marchand
Vice President, Partner Solutions

It would be hard to dream, think and write about being resilient from a point of theory. There have been many along the way who have shaped, guided and journeyed with me as I've walked my own journey into resilience, which I am still walking. My joy and gratefulness are overwhelming for the following incomplete list of people ...

Erin, my amazing wife. We don't often express our affection for one another on public platforms, but you are my best friend and biggest fan. You are a constant reminder to me that God gives really, really good gifts! I am the luckiest. I love you. I love you. I love you.

Griffin, Elin, Amelia and Lucia, you are four of my favorite faces and my greatest of treasures. I hope and pray you always know there is and will always be a church, and a people to whom you belong. It may not always be easy, they may not always be kind, but they are your brothers and sisters, the church needs you, and you need them. You are a part of 2050 and beyond. I'm so excited to see the dreams God has for each of you and the amazing leaders you're growing up to be. Lead, in Jesus, with conviction, compassion, creativity and courage.

For my fellow writers: Valerie, you are an amazing, visionary leader! You are the Wendy for us Lost Boys and the open door for nobody's children. You have the courage of a warrior and the soul of an artist. Thank you for inviting me to the dance. Matt, you are my brother. Truly. I'm better for having you in my life. My gratitude for our friendship escapes any and all words I possess. Chris, you are true grit. I am in true admiration of your tenacity and love for the Church. YOU. ARE. A. TRUE. JEDI!

The team at Awana, I am so amazed I get to serve with you all. You're among the most creative, get-it-done, courageous group of women and men on the planet. Kevin White, I couldn't imagine taking on this mission without you, nor would I want to. You are a generous, wise and amazing friend and you sharpen me, always. Diego and Michelle, you amaze me! You bring creativity and beauty to everything. Kendra, we would have been lost a long time ago without you ... sorry for any and all grey hairs I may have caused. Cindy, Chip, Brian, Ken, Deb and Deby, can you all believe we're here? Always better together! Thank you all, let's keep going!

There are others who speak love and truth into my life and show me the love of Jesus. Kevin O., Sean and Jeremy, you are my brothers and each of you shape me in different ways. Steve, let's light a fire sometime soon, I'm ALWAYS up for it!

Mike Handler
Chief Communications Officer

GLOSSARY

Resilient *(adj: resilient)*

A quality describing the spiritual elasticity of a child or adult. The resistant strength to bend and flex, but not break against the weight of culture.

Synonyms: *strong, tough, hardy, quick to recover, quick to bounce back, buoyant, difficult to keep down, irrepressible, adaptable, flexible*

Child Disciple: A child who loves Jesus for the rest of his or her life.

Church Babies: A child or children cared for by the entire church, no matter their family situation.

Discipleship: The process of belonging to, believing in and becoming like Jesus Christ.

Fire Carriers: A term from the days of the pioneers in American history. The fire carrier would be responsible for housing and transferring the embers of a fire from one camp to another. The meaning here is rich, and for our purposes describes one who transfers light, warmth, truth, safety and more from one generation to another.

Identity: Understanding, believing and living out whom God says I am.

KidMin: A broad or generalized short-hand term for kid's ministry or children's ministry. It could mean any ministry for kids from Sunday school, to VBS, to a midweek ministry.

Loving, Caring Adult: This is a vital leader in children's or youth ministry that allows a child the ability to belong. This individual understands that each kid matters and exhibits love by knowing a child's name, looking her/him in the eye, praising their efforts and making sure each child knows they are loved, known and cared for by Jesus and His church. This position could be a coach, mentor, teacher, church leader, etc.

Radical Love: Going beyond what's expected to a wholistic defining way of relating to a generation of kids. Leading and engaging beyond the expected requirements of ministry and loving kids beyond a surface-level engagement.

Resilient Child Discipleship: The process of a Christ follower committing meaningful, intentional and consistent time and space to a child or a group of children so that they may know who Jesus is, are known by a body of believers (Belong), to place their faith in Jesus, apply the Word of God (Believe) and to reproduce their own discipleship (Become), so that a third spiritual generation can lead and love like Jesus Christ.

Spine and Heart: The ability to stand with conviction and compassion in the face of adversity. Not compromising truth and not failing to love others no matter the belief. Often times, when facing adversity, one should start with building a bridge of understanding and empathy prior to presenting biblical viewpoints. It is approaching with grace and understanding, then truth, in that order.

2050: While we are defining a year or point in time, 2050 is really a term we're using to talk about the future.

3B: Belong, Believe, Become: The 3B ministry philosophy is at the heart of the Awana approach to ministry, both in the US and around the world. It focuses on the three movements of discipleship (see below) from pre-conversion to discipleship. We have seen it bear good fruit for over 70 years.

> **BELONG** – Highly relational ministry, led by loving and caring adults.

> **BELIEVE** – Deeply Scriptural ministry, rooted in the truth of God's Word and the power of the gospel.

> **BECOME** – Truly experiential ministry, designed to move kids from simulation to real-world application of faith-based living.

NOTES

CHAPTER 1

[1] Awana is a global discipleship ministry to children. At the time of publication Awana is ministering in 122 countries through 60,664 clubs to 4.8 million children.

[2] Barna Group, *Faith For Exiles: 5 Ways for a New Generation to Follow Jesus in Digital Babylon* (Grand Rapids, MI: Baker Books, 2019)

[3] Ed Stetzer, *Christians in the Age of Outrage: How to Bring Our Best When the World is at It's Worst* (Carol Stream, IL: Tyndale House, 2018)

[4] Barna Group, *Faith for Exiles: 5 Ways for a New Generation to Follow Jesus in Digital Babylon* (Grand Rapids, MI: Baker Books, 2019), 64

[5] Ibid.,64.

[6] Ibid., 32.

[7] Ed Stetzer, *Christians in the Age of Outrage: How to Bring Our Best When the World is at It's Worst* (Carol Stream, IL: Tyndale House, 2018), 29.

CHAPTER 2

[1] David Kinnaman and Mark Matlock, *Faith For Exiles; 5 Ways for a New Generation to Follow Jesus in Digital Babylon* (Grand Rapids, MI: Baker Books, 2019), 91.

[2] Meghan Cox Gurdon, *The Enchanted Hour* (New York: HarperCollins, 2019), 13, 14.

[3] Vicky Rideout, Sita Pai, "U.S. Teens Use an Average of Nine Hours of Media Per Day, Tweenz Use Six Hours," Common Sense Media, November 3, 2015, 13.

4   Meghan Cox Gurdon, *The Enchanted Hour* (New York: HarperCollins, 2019), 13,14.

5   Jean M. Twenge et al., "Decreases in Psychological Well-Being among American Adolescents after 2012 and Links to Screen Time during the Rise of Smart Phone Technology," Emotion, January 22, 2018.

6   Ed Stetzer, *Christians in the Age of Outrage: How to Bring Our Best When the World is at It's Worst* (Carol Stream: Tyndale House, 2018), 33.

7   *Time Flies: U.SD. "Adults Now Spend Nearly Half a Day Interacting With Media,"* First Quarter Nielsen Total Audience Report, July, 31, 2018.

8   Wayne Parker, *"Statistics About Children of Divorce,"* https://verywellfamily.com.

9   *"GenZ: Your Questions Answered,"*-Barna Group, https://www.barna.com>research.genzquestionsanswered.

10   Kara Powell, https://fulleryouthinstitute.org/stickyfaith.

11   Thom Rainer, https://factsandtrends.net/hopefordyingchurches

12   Barna Update, *"Most Twentysomethings Put Christianity on the Shelf Following Spiritually Active Teen Years,"* https://Barna.com

13   Ed Stetzer, *"Drops Outs and Disciples: How many students are really leaving the church?"* https://christianitytoday.com

14   David Kinnaman & Mark Matllock, *Faith for Exiles: 5 Ways for a New Generation to Follow Jesus in Digital Babylon* (Grand Rapids: Baker Books, 2019), 32.

15   https://www.pewforum.org/religious-landscape-study/attendance-at-religious-services/

16   David Kinnaman & Mark Matllock, *Faith for Exiles: 5 Ways for a New Generation to Follow Jesus in Digital Babylon* (Grand Rapids: Baker Books, 2019), 98.

CHAPTER 3

1   Frederick Buechner, *Wishful Thinking: A Theological ABC* (San Francisco: Harper & Row, 1973), 2.

2   RussVought, https://www.theresurgent.com/wheatoncollegeandthepreservationoftheologicalclarity

3   David French, "Watch Bernie Sanders Attack a Christian Nominee and Impose an Unconstitutional Religious Test for Public Office," *The National Review*, May 17, 2019.

4   On February 28, 2018 in a 50-49 vote Russell Vought was confirmed by the Senate for Deputy Director of the Office of Management and Budget office

5   https://www.huffpost.com/entry/is-the-church-dying_b_8498804

6   https://www.christianitytoday.com/news/2019/march/evangelical- nones-mainline-us-general-social-survey-gss.html

7   Alex Daniels, "Religious Americans Give More, New Study Finds," The Chronicle of Philanthropy, November 25, 2013. https://www.ecfa.org/content/2017state-of-giving-report

8   John Ortberg, *Who is This Man?* (Grand Rapids: Zondervan, 2012), 7 foreword. Two books that excellently contrast the pagan pre- Jesus world with the post-Jesus world and his impact on the live of women and children are: John Ortberg, *Who Is This Man?: The Unpredictable Impact of the Inescapable Jesus* (GrandRapids: Zondervan, 2012) And Thomas Cahill, *The Desire of the Everlasting Hills: The World Before and After Jesus* (New York: Doubleday, 1990)

9   Dinesh D'Souza, *What's So Great About Christianity?* (Washington DC: Regnery Publishing, 2007), 299.

10   Colossians 3: 5,8, 12. NIV

CHAPTER 4

[1]   Shawn Thornton, *All But Normal: Life on Victory Road* (Wheaton, Tyndale House Publishers, 2016), 275.

[2]   Ibid.

[3]   Albert Mohler, The Future of the Southern Baptist Convention: The Numbers Don't Add Up. albertmohler.com

CHAPTER 5

[1]   Bobette Buster *Do Story: How to tell your story so the world listens.* Pg 1.

[2]   https://christianhistoryinstitute.org/magazine/article/see-how-these-christians-love

[3]   https://www.nytimes.com/2019/09/19/magazine/poem-small- kindnesses.html

CHAPTER 6

[1]   https://www.developingchild.harvard.edu/supportive-relationships-and-skill-building-strengthen-the-foundations-of-resilience

[2]   Ibid.

[3]   https://www.theguardian.com/society/2019/apr/27/technology-threatens-child-development-psychology-expert-warns

[4]   David Kinnaman and Mark Matlock, *Faith for Exiles: 5 Ways for a New Generation to Follow Jesus in Digital Babylon* (Grand Rapids: Baker Books, 2019), 36, 37.

[5]   Ibid. 54.

CHAPTER 7

1   Kara E. Powell and Dr. Chap Clark, *Sticky Faith* (Grand Rapids: Zondervan, 2011), 101.

CHAPTER 8

1   Matt Markins, Dan Lovaglia, Mark McPeak, *The Gospel Truth About Children's Ministry* (Streamwood: Awana, 2014), 33.

2   Ibid. 53.

3   David Kinnaman and Mark Matlock, Faith For Exiles: *5 Ways for a New Generation to Follow Jesus in a Digital Babylon* (Grand Rapids: Baker Books, 2019), 33

4   Greg McKeown, *Essentialism: The Disciplined Pursuit of Less* (New York: Crown Business, 2014)

5   https//seths.blog/2015/10/infrastructure/

CHAPTER 9

1   https://www.apa.org/helpcenter/road-resilience

2   Southwick, Steven M., and Dennis S. Charney. *Resilience the Science of Mastering Life's Greatest Challenges.* Cambridge University Press, 2018, 10.

3   Ibid.,15.

4   Ibid.,16.

5   INBRIEF: *The Science of Resilience,* The Center on the Developing Child of Harvard University, 1

6   Southwick, Steven M., and Dennis S. Charney. *Resilience the Science of Mastering Life's Greatest Challenges.* Cambridge University Press, 2018., 158.

CHAPTER 10

1   https://www.theguardian.com/news/datablog/2010/feb/01/nasa-budgets-us-spending-space-travel

2   Cited in Steve J. Dick, "Why We Explore," http://www.nasa.gov/exploration/whyweexplore/Why_We_29.html.

3   George Barna, *Transforming Children Into Spiritual Champions* (Ventura: Regal Books, 2003), 78.

4   Kara E. Powell and Chap Clark, *Sticky Faith: Everyday Ideas to Build Lasting Faith in Your Kids* (Grand Rapids: Zondervan, 2011), 71.

5   Awana October 2019 Research Project. Page 62

6   Smith, Christian and Snell, Patricia. *Souls in Transition: The religious and spiritual lives of emerging adults.* (2009). New York, NY: Oxford University Press. p. 227.

7   Brown, Brené. 2015. *Daring greatly: how the courage to be vulnerable transforms the way we live, love, parent, and lead.* New York, NY. Avery. 231-232.

8   Kara E. Powell and Chap Clark, Sticky Faith: Everyday Ideas to Build Lasting Faith in Your Kids (Grand Rapids: Zondervan, 2011), 99.

9   Ibid.97.

10   https://www.childtrends.org/wp-content/uploads/2013/12/2013-54CaringAdults.pdf

11   https://link.springer.com/article/10.1007/s10560-005-2546-4

12   https://link.springer.com/article/10.1007/s10560-005-2546-4

[1] http://lifewayresearch.com/wp-content/uploads/2017/10/kids-influencers-final.jpg

[1] https://lifewayresearch.com/2017/10/17/young-bible-readers-more- likely-to-be-faithful-adults-study-finds/

[1] https://www.barna.com/research/evangelism-is-most-effective-among-kids/

[1] David Kinnaman and Mark Matlock, *Faith for Exiles: 5 Ways for a New Generation to Follow Jesus in a Digital Babylon* (Grand Rapids: Baker Books, 2019), 44

[1] https://www.barna.com/research/state-of-the-bible-2018-seven-top-findings/

[1] Matt Markins, Dan Lovaglia, and Mark McPeak, *The Gospel Truth About Children's Ministry* (Streamwood: Awana, 2015), 29.

[1] *Ibid, 30.*

[1] Kara E. Powell and Chap Clark, *Sticky Faith: Everyday Ideas to Build Lasting Faith in Your Kids* (Grand Rapids: Zondervan, 2011),129.

[1] https://www.barna.com/research/parents-and-pastors-partners-in-gen-z-discipleship/

[1] https://www.barna.com/research/parents-and-pastors-partners-in-gen-z-discipleship/

[1] *Sticky Faith: Everyday Ideas to Build Lasting Faith in Your Kids*, Dr. Kara E. Powell & Dr. Chap Clark, Page 98

[1] *Sticky Faith: Everyday Ideas to Build Lasting Faith in Your Kids*, Dr. Kara E. Powell & Dr. Chap Clark, Page 131, 135, 146

CHAPTER 11

[1] https://www.lausanne.org/.best-of-lausanne/developing-disciples-jesus-way-audio

CHAPTER 12

[1] John Rinehart, Gospel Patrons: *People Whose Generosity Changed The World*, Reclaimed Publishing, 2013

VALERIE BELL

Chief Executive Officer

Valerie Bell is the CEO and 2050 vision caster for Awana, a global leader in child discipleship. She has authored eight books including: *Nobody's Children, Getting Out of Your Kids' Faces and Into Their Hearts* and *Faith-Shaped Kids.* She and her husband, Steve, have two grown, resilient sons and six amazing grandchildren.

REV. CHRIS MARCHAND

Vice President of Partner Solutions

Chris is the Vice President of Partner Solutions at Awana. Chris and his wife, Tricia, have two daughters. They share a love for strong coffee, crispy bacon, Sci-fi movies, and spending their date nights at the library or antiquing.

MATT MARKINS

President, Chief Strategy Officer

Matt Markins is President and Chief Strategy Officer at Awana. He speaks publicly on organizational leadership and child discipleship. He is the coauthor of two other books, *Leading Kidmin: How to Drive Real Change in Children's Ministry* and *The Gospel Truth About Children's Ministry*. He and his wife, Katie are lifelong children's ministry advocates, pull for the Tennessee Titans, and have two teenage sons.

MIKE HANDLER

Chief Communications Officer

Mike Handler is the Chief Communications Officer at Awana. He has 18 years of experience in business and ministry, including pastoring, church planting, and leading his own design and strategy group. Through engaging storytelling and collaboration, he helps leaders understand the culture and creatively solve problems. Mike and his wife, Erin, have four children. They love traveling, making breakfast and cheering on the Cubs and Bears.